Cassie's Tale

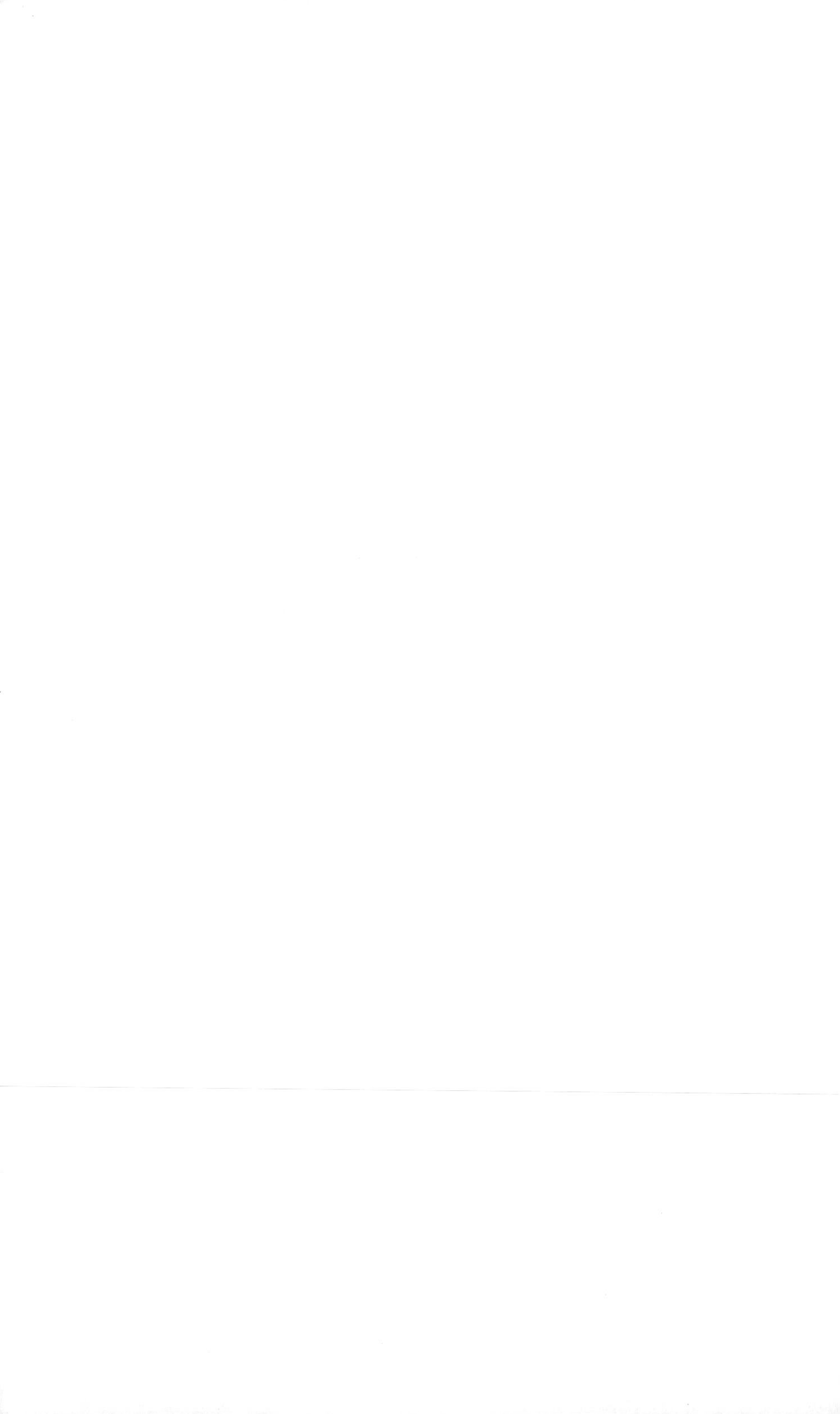

Cassie's Tale

or
Rescuing the 'Mad Ferret'

Brian L Porter

Published 2018 by Creativia

Acknowledgements

Before I commence with Cassie's Tale, I feel it necessary to say a few words of thanks to people who have made this book possible. If it wasn't for my publisher, Miika Hannila at Creativia Publishing, none of my dog rescue books and thrillers would be here for you, my readers to enjoy, so it's a great big thank you to Miika for all his support for my work over the years. I also owe a big debt of gratitude to my researcher and proof reader, Debbie Poole. Debbie has spent many hours going through each chapter of the book in her efforts to help make it as accurate and as entertaining as possible. Without her help and hard work, my books wouldn't be as polished as they are by the time they reach my publisher.

I owe a very special debt of gratitude to Rebecca Aldren, Cassie's vet, and the Practice Manager at the Doncaster branch of Vets for Pets. Over the years, she has always provided Cassie, and all our dogs, particularly our epileptic 'superdog' Sasha with the best possible care and she (and her wonderful staff of vets, nurses and reception staff) have always gone out of their way to help and advise us of the best courses of action to take when any of our dogs has required veterinary treatment. Thank you to everyone of you. I'm sorry there are too many of you to name each one of you here, but you all have mine and Juliet's love and gratitude for all you do for our pets, who as you all know, mean the world to us.

My wife Juliet must receive my thanks too. Not only is she responsible for the daily grooming and general care of the dogs, but she spends many hours every day of her life walking miles in the process of making sure our dogs are fully exercised and given the opportunity to run and play. The only dogs she doesn't walk are Sasha, who for some reason will only walk with me and Sheba, who is now old and arthritic and joins me and Sasha on our more restricted walks. All I can say is that it's no wonder Juliet is so fit and in such great shape. She's living proof that walking is good for you!

Finally, my thanks go to all my readers, especially those who read Sasha and Sheba's life stories and helped to turn them into bestsellers along the way. It is you, through various modes of contact who have asked me repeatedly to tell the story of how Cassie came to be a part of our family of rescues. This then, is Cassie's Tale, and it's especially for you, dear readers, all of you.

Contents

Chapter 1

In the Beginning

It's only right that I begin Cassie's story by telling you something of her life before she became a part of our rescue family. By the time she joined us, she had already had three previous owners, in the first two years of her life.

It began, to the best of our knowledge when our friend, Linda, was walking her dogs one dark and rainy night, and she heard cries and whimpering coming from the direction of the garden of a house she was walking past. Being naturally inquisitive, Linda stopped to try and discover where the plaintive noises were originating from. She actually climbed the wall into the garden and there she discovered the source of the whimpering and crying, a tiny, wet and bedraggled, shivering little pup, with nowhere to go to get out of the rain. Linda was furious that someone had left the little pup outdoors in such terrible weather conditions and she knocked on the door of the house for quite some time until the door was finally opened.

God only knows what the man who answered the door must have thought when he was suddenly confronted by this strange woman, wearing weatherproof coat and hood, with two dogs at her side and his puppy in the crook of her arm. She must have resembled a cross between Freddy Krueger and The Grim Reaper, especially when she launched into a tirade about his treatment of the puppy, (Linda pulls no punches when it comes to defending animals, I promise you). The way she told it, she asked him what the hell he was thinking, leaving that poor little dog out in the rain. She told him he didn't deserve to have a dog, to which he replied, "I never wanted the thing in the first place."

Linda's instant response was, "Can I take it home with me then, and find it a good home?"

"Take it if you want it," he replied, so she did, after first getting what details she could from him about the dog and getting him to sign a note saying he'd given up the dog to her.

She learned that the dog's name was Cassie, and that she was around twelve weeks old, and was a Yorkshire Terrier/Australian Terrier crossbreed. With that, she led little Cassie away to what she hoped would soon be a better life. Linda's other dogs, Jet and Diesel, welcomed the tiny terrier into their home and it didn't take Cassie long to dry out and feel the warmth of Linda's home beginning to make her feel more like a twelve-week-old puppy should do. The very next day, she arrived on the field, where the regular group of dog walkers gathered every afternoon and Cassie was introduced to everyone. Linda would very much have liked to keep Cassie, but the terms of her home rental only allowed her to keep two pets and she already had two dogs and two cats, so was pushing things a bit already. So, she let it be known that she was looking for a good home for Cassie, and within a few weeks she told us that Cassie was going to live with an elderly couple who lived on her street. Nobody on the field knew the couple but Linda was sure they would give the little dog a good home. Time, however would prove otherwise, as my story will reveal, but for now, as far as everyone was concerned, Cassie was happy and on the way to a good future with her new owners.

Chapter 2

Summer 2007

"What's that," I asked, as Juliet stepped from the car and walked down our garden path towards the front door, looking slightly furtive, semi-pregnant, with a bulge in her grooming jacket that failed to hide the very small head peeking out from under her arm.

"It's a dog," was her sheepish reply, delivered with an almost guilty grin.

Now, I may be many things, but blind isn't one of them. I may wear glasses, and my eyesight is nowhere near perfect, but even I couldn't fail to recognise the small creature that she was apparently trying to smuggle into the house, that warm sunny, summer's day in 2007.

"I can see it's a dog, but what's it doing here?" I asked. Of course, as Juliet and I spent our lives rescuing dogs and giving them new forever homes, I should have caught on straight away, or, maybe I did, and just wanted to tease her a little. I mean, did she really think I wouldn't notice another dog running around in the house?

Before I go on, maybe I should explain a little about the circumstances behind Juliet's sudden appearance that day, with the dog tucked underneath her arm. Back in 2007, Juliet was doing pretty well, having recently begun her own mobile dog grooming business. She had a few regular clients and it was her fervent hope that she would be able to build her clientele substantially until she was able to really make a go of things as a dog groomer, having completed a course to gain her qualification. We were unaware, at that time, that she would later be struck by carpel tunnel syndrome that would destroy her dream. That day, she had set off to a neighbouring village to groom a little terrier, one of her regulars at that time. This was the dog that had once been owned by our friend, Linda, who had been instrumental in rescuing her from the appalling conditions she was living in. Although Linda later gave the dog to an elderly neighbour, soon afterwards, the neighbour and her husband announced that they were moving home and going to live in a sheltered accommodation bungalow in a nearby village. Linda thus waved goodbye to little Cassie, as she departed for her new home some weeks later.

It was about a year later that Juliet first received the call to go and groom little Cassie and she regularly visited the little terrier in her new home in the coming months until that fateful day when she arrived home with the dog tucked into her jacket.

So, having asked her what the dog was doing here at our home when of course she'd only gone to groom her, Juliet now replied to my question.

"The lady didn't want her and asked if I'd like to take her. She knows we take in rescue dogs and she told me she couldn't walk Cassie properly any more. She uses a disability scooter to get around and can only take Cassie on her lead, attached to the scooter, for short trips and that's not ideal. Where they live, it's all open plan, so she can't even let her out to run around in the back garden because it's a communal area and the neighbours would complain. On top of all that, her husband hates the dog."

"How can anyone hate a little thing like that?" I asked, softening to the idea of adding Cassie to our family.

"Honestly, Brian, you should have seen him. He's a bit of a slob, sat in a chair, watching daytime TV and never even looked up to acknowledge me when I went in to groom the dog, and when his wife told him Cassie was leaving with me (she must have planned this in advance), and asked him to say goodbye to the little dog, he didn't turn around or look at her, and just said 'Goodbye dog.' He didn't care about Cassie at all or that his wife was upset at letting her go. She at least wanted what was best for Cassie and knew it wasn't the right place for her, being with them. When I walked out of the bungalow, she came to the car with me and Cassie and whispered to me that her husband detested the dog, saying that it wasn't the kind of dog a man would want to be seen with, the pompous git."

I personally detest people with attitudes like the man she described and that really swayed my opinion into accepting that Cassie was moving in with us.

"You'd better take her out from your jacket then and let's have a good look at her," I said, as Juliet slowly extricated Cassie from her jacket. I remembered Cassie vaguely from when Linda owned her but now, in close-up, I realised how tiny she was. Barely twelve inches long, she was a grey haired, little terrier with a long tail that curled upwards and with white 'socks' on the bottom of her paws. Because Juliet had just given her a good summer clip, she appeared to have 'tiger stripes' in her coat, with pretty golden stripes under her upper grey coat. In truth, she was a very tiny dog and we later found out from Linda she was an unusual crossbreed, between a Yorkshire Terrier and an Australian Terrier. Juliet further explained that Cassie was two and a half years old, though due to her size and unbridled energy, anyone could be forgiven for thinking she was a puppy of a few months of age.

"Let's get her indoors then, and see what the others think of her," I said as we went through the gate and took Cassie into the garden where most of our other dogs were lying in the sunshine. Whether it was because she was so small, I don't know, but the other dogs barely noticed her at first. Back in 2007, the make-up of our rescue pack was very different to today. There was no Sasha, Digby, Muffin or Petal, and no Sheba, Dexter or Muttley. Our 'pack leader' was Tilly, a highly intelligent, scruffy little Bedlington/Glen of Imaal Terrier crossbreed, who quickly took Cassie under her wing. They were both of similar colour, but Tilly was taller and longer and in fact, Cassie's best friend in those early days was Sophie, our lovely brindle coloured whippet/lurcher. The only dogs we owned in those days who are still with us are Dylan and Penny. Dylan has been with us longer than any of the other dogs, having been with us for thirteen years. What great fun Cassie and Sophie shared together, running free on the local playing field, playing with a tennis ball. The pair even devised their own game, with them cleverly dropping the ball from mouth to mouth and then chasing each other around the field, finally dropping the ball at my feet for me to throw for them to begin their game all over again.

So, for the next few weeks, Cassie gradually integrated herself into our rescue pack, and we began to see more and more of her personality. Despite being so small, Cassie was a little powerhouse, with an attitude to match. She took no nonsense from any of the other dogs, all of whom were larger than she was, and they all learned to give Cassie the respect she deserved. She slept in a bed in the kitchen with the majority of the pack, and woe betide any dog who tried to disturb her beauty sleep! They would get the full 'Cassie treatment' of her shrill little bark as if to say, *"Go away and stop bugging my happiness."*

As the weeks turned into months, we were left in no doubt that Cassie had fully integrated herself into our family of rescue dogs, and life was good for all concerned.

Sophie and Cassie

Chapter 3

Training

It seems a long time ago now, but when Cassie first joined us, I would regularly disappear from home on Saturday afternoon with a number of our dogs in the back of the car, to go to our regular dog training session, which took place a few miles away, under the auspices of one of the north of England's leading canine behaviourists, who I'd met some years earlier and who had helped us tremendously in sorting out what we thought was bad behaviour being exhibited by Tilly. We were surprised to discover, thanks to Brian, (yes, we shared the same first name), that Tilly wasn't a bad dog at all. She was so intelligent, that what we took for bad behaviour was simply her way of exhibiting boredom! Brian had quickly identified the fact that Tilly needed challenging on an intellectual level and before long, with the benefit of a few sessions at this dog training classes, she became the star of his classes. She loved taking part in agility classes, and before long she was the fastest dog in the class, and, most surprisingly, she became the only dog that could negotiate the course without a handler, (me) at her side. Over time, Tilly went on to set several record times which, to my knowledge, have never been beaten. Flyball came next, but wasn't really her forte, as she loved tennis balls so much, she was reluctant to give it up at the end of the run. Tilly's greatest achievement really came when Brian decided she had the ability and intelligence to learn to be a search and rescue dog. She gradually learned to track a scent, first of all being able to locate an object hidden at ground level, and then moving on to items hidden off the ground in trees etc. The pinnacle of her search training came when she was able to recognise and locate items that bore the scent of human DNA. She was one clever dog!

So, when training day came around, our two girls would join me, and we would regularly take Tilly, Charlie the Cairn terrier, Molly the Westie, and Cassie along to the training classes. Now, while Tilly showed off her quite incredible skills, the others never quite hit those heights, but the whole idea of the training was for the dogs to have fun as they learned, and we had some great laughs as the others did their best at agility or search and rescue and so on. Charlie, Molly and Cassie had to be led over the agility obstacles while on the lead. We did try letting Cassie do the course off-lead once, but it then took me and the girls and a few of the other owners about five minutes to catch her as she ran around the training field at top speed, having the time of her life, running up to and teasing the other dogs in the class, who stood patiently beside their owners, politely waiting their turn.

Everyone laughed at Cassie's antics as she powered her way round and round the field like a miniature whirling dervish, or, as someone put it, a one-dog tsunami! That was the last time she was allowed on the agility course without a lead on.

Occasionally we would vary the dogs that would accompany Tilly on her Saturday afternoons at training, and once she joined the pack, Cassie's best pal Sophie would often come along to keep her friend company. They looked so incongruous together, the long legged, tall rangy lurcher and the tiny little crossbreed terrier.

Of course, all good things come to an end, and as our two girls, Rebecca and Victoria grew older they eventually lost their interest in accompanying me and the dogs to the training sessions, and gradually our attendance on the Saturdays diminished until it became impossible to continue. There was no way I could continue to take three or four dogs on my own so with regret, the dog training sessions came to an end. It's worth mentioning that by that time the word 'training' wasn't appropriate as our dogs were fully trained and we were really just going along for the fun of it. I know Tilly missed it more than most, as she seemed to know whenever Saturday came around and would be ready and waiting, getting excited, as lunchtime came around.

Still, there was no way Cassie was any less energetic. Everyone who met her was astounded at the speed at which this little girl could run and the way she would keep going at full speed from beginning to the end of her walks. When released on the playing field, she would literally begin running at breakneck speed, and would keep it up until it was time to go home. She ran for the sheer pleasure of it, her ears pricked up, her tail held high over her back and her tongue lolling out as if she was totally out of breath, which, of course, she never seemed to get. Cassie was quickly proving herself to be quite a little character, no more so than the day when, as Juliet took her out one day, they bumped into Linda, her first owner, who was of course delighted to see little Cassie again. Cassie however, did her best to ignore Linda, something she does very well when she is focussed on going for a run, and both Juliet and Linda ended up having a good laugh at Cassie's 'ignorant' behaviour. As hard as Linda tried, there was no way Cassie was going to stand still and allow herself to be fussed over.

Cassie found it difficult to allow people to get too close to her or let them stroke or fuss her. Perhaps it had something to do with the way she'd been treated by her original owner, or maybe there were facts we were unaware of about the way she'd been treated and ignored by the man with whom she'd lived prior to coming to us. There was one person though, who found a way to get Cassie close to her, and we'll close this chapter now and move on to the day Cassie met her new best friend.

Dog training 2007

Chapter 4

Cindy

We had quite a good routine in those early years of Cassie's time with us. This meant that most of the time, she would spend her walks (should I call them runs?), going to the smaller of the two playing fields in the village with me, Tilly, Molly and Sophie. It was on that field one day that we met the lady and the little dog who was to become Cassie's best friend, outside of our own pack.

While walking and playing with my dogs on the field, I'd often seen a lady in the distance, walking a little Yorkshire Terrier. I noticed that the little dog was always on the lead and the lady always went out of her way to avoid anyone with other dogs. One morning, I was playing with the dogs as usual when Cassie suddenly turned and ran across the field, straight towards the lady with the Yorkie.

Oops, I thought, and called my other dogs to me and set off in the direction Cassie had taken. As we drew closer, I could see the lady was standing still with her little dog at her feet and Cassie was bouncing up and down in front of her.

"Don't worry," I called once we were in talking range. "She won't hurt your dog."

The lady didn't quite look convinced at first, but, as we got even closer and Tilly, Molly and Sophie didn't make any moves towards her dog, she calmed down a little.

"I'm Brian," I introduced myself, "and this is Tilly, Molly and Sophie. The little bundle of joy in front of you is Cassie."

"This is Cindy," she replied. "I'm Maureen."

"Hello, Maureen, nice to meet you. I've often seen you here but guessed your Cindy is a bit nervous."

"She was attacked once when she was a puppy and has always been scared of other dogs since then."

"She doesn't seem too scared of Cassie," I said, watching as Cindy slowly began wagging her tail as Cassie inched ever nearer to her.

Before long, Cassie was jumping up and down in front of Cindy and Cindy was furiously wagging her tail in a display of friendship. I quickly called Cassie back to me and clipped her lead on to her collar. We then spent about twenty minutes walking round the perimeter of the field with Maureen and Cindy and slowly, the little Yorkie appeared to look and act more confidently with all my dogs, who were all so well behaved and after saying a quick doggie 'hello' to her, each of them carried on walking peacefully at my side. Maureen was impressed with how well my dogs were trained and asked if she could walk Cindy with us again the next day.

The next day soon turned into every day and then the great day came when Maureen, in response to my regular pleading, finally agreed to let Cindy off her lead. I was certain my dogs would be okay with her and reassured her of the fact as she tentatively released Cindy, for the first time in years. In a way, those first few seconds of seeing Cindy off the lead were quite funny, as, instead of running away, or even walking around, she just stood still, not moving at all, as if she didn't quite realise or understand she was free to move around as she wished.

Predictably, it was Cassie who finally got Cindy moving. She began bouncing around in front of Cindy, going into a play crouch, and then turning and running a short distance away from her, where she stood, barking her little high-pitched bark as if to say, *"Come on then. What are you waiting for?"* Suddenly, Cindy seemed to catch on, and slowly, she trotted to where Cassie stood, waiting for her. As soon as she drew close, Cassie would turn and run a little further, gradually encouraging Cindy to follow her and moving her further away from her 'mum' Maureen. All the time this was going on, my other dogs were happily entertaining themselves, running around the field, bringing their tennis balls to me so I could throw them for them to chase and retrieve while Cassie was having fun with her new friend.

After a few minutes of tentative sparring it appeared as if Cindy suddenly found her confidence. This time, when Cassie did her play crouch and runaway, to our delight, Cindy ran after her. Cassie seemed equally surprised. Next thing, the pair were chasing one another all over the place. Cindy was a joy to behold as years of not being allowed to run free seemed to melt away as she immersed herself in the joy of playing 'chase' with her new-found friend. When Cassie ran to me and began to jump up and down like a jack in the box, (her way of asking for her ball) I duly obliged her and took her ball from my pocket and threw it for her. She took off after the ball and Cindy went with her. The two of them, being roughly the same size, made a great couple of playmates and between themselves they seemed to devise their own way of playing with the ball, passing it between them on the ground by nudging it with their noses. So, the game that Maureen and I were to call 'nose tennis' was born, invented by two little terriers who had found their own way of having fun with a tennis ball.

From that day onwards, Cindy would become a great friend to all the dogs in our pack, and Tilly and Sophie in particular acted very protectively towards her, so lovely to see. Maureen was adamant though, that she would only let Cindy off-lead when she was with me and my dogs. This made sense, bearing in mind what had happened to Cindy in the past and as long as I was there with my dogs, she was surrounded by protection and could be confident and playful. Maureen too, gradually grew to love my dogs who had been instrumental in giving new life to her beloved Yorkie, and as we met twice a day, morning and afternoon on the playing field with our dogs, Cindy was never short of play mates and doggie fun.

Cassie and Cindy's friendship would endure for many years. It was only a change in my health circumstances and the fact that as our girls grew older and found going out with the dogs less attractive than going out with their friends that it became unworkable for me to take four dogs at a time on the playing field and our time with Cindy gradually tapered off, much to our disappointment. But, that was the future and at the time we are talking about, this was all new and exciting for Cindy and for me and my dogs too.

Every dog walk was a joy and a pleasure and I never failed to go home with a smile on my face, and my dogs all had energetically wagging tails on their way home. Cassie's arrival had not only been good for her, but had brought new life to another little dog. Cindy would very soon become an honorary member of our pack. After all, she spent most of her time with us!

Cassie and Cindy, 2012

Chapter 5

Another New Friend

A lot of new things seemed to correspond to Cassie's arrival, none more so than the arrival of another new member of our little pack of rescues. One day, while I was visiting the vets to have one of our dogs' annual booster injection carried out, Lisa, one of the veterinary receptionists, knowing of my record of rescuing dogs in need, 'just happened' to ask me if I knew of anybody who might be willing to take a little terrier in, and give it a new home. I wasn't aware up until that day that Lisa was herself a dog breeder. She bred and sold Dogue de Bordeaux puppies. She explained to me that because she was known as the 'dog lady' among the local children in the village where she lived, it had been almost fated that when some of those children found a little pup, they wold take it to her.

Due to space restrictions, she explained that she had taken the little dog in, but had no room to give it a permanent home. She already had three dogs of her own in the house, in addition to her breeding animals. She had looked after the little terrier for some months, but had been unable up to then, to find a suitable new home for her. She wasn't the sort of person to just give the dog to 'anyone' and was meticulous in trying to find the right home for her long-term temporary guest. I think she knew we were just the people to take the pup, who by then was, she guessed, about eighteen months old.

Using my ancient old faithful Nokia phone, I called Juliet at home and we agreed to at least take a look at the dog to see if we thought it would fit into our pack and our home. I made arrangements with Lisa, who gave me her address which I was pleased to hear was in a village only five miles from our home, so it wasn't far to travel. As she was still at work, Lisa couldn't give me all the details about the dog, who she'd named Pancake, as it had been Shrove Tuesday, pancake day, when the children who'd found her had handed the little pup in to Lisa. I agreed to go and see the dog that evening after she'd finished work when she could tell us whatever we wanted to know about the 'mystery' terrier.

It was a beautiful, warm sunny evening when Juliet and I arrived at Lisa's home. What appeared, from the outside to be a small, traditional terraced home, turned into something else when Lisa invited us in and took us through the house and into the back garden. The garden gave way onto a large field, which Lisa explained she owned as well as her house. Two horses were peacefully grazing in the field and over to one side were Lisa's purpose-built kennels. She spent a few minutes showing us round and also introduced us to her own dogs, which included a Bedlington Terrier, very like our own Dylan, but much larger. Her dog hadn't had the terrible start in life that Dylan had suffered and it made us realise just how undersized our little Bedlington was as a result of poor care and feeding in his early months of life.

Finally, she asked us to wait while she went to bring the reason for our visit to meet us. She disappeared into the kennels and a couple of minutes later she reappeared, with a little black and white terrier running alongside her. The dog she'd called Pancake was clearly a happy and cheerful little character who ran past us and picked up a deflated football that lay on the ground and began running around with it in her mouth, her tail wagging as she ran.

We watched her at play for a couple of minutes and then Lisa called her over to us and she came straight away and allowed us to make a big fuss of her. Juliet and I then spent a few minutes taking it in turns to play with the little dog who looked like a Jack Russell crossed with...something else! We neither knew not cared about her ancestry. All that mattered to us was that she looked as though she'd fit in perfectly with our happy band of rescue dogs.

Lisa was now able to tell us the full story about how Pancake came to be with her. Apparently, a group of gypsies had made camp near the village railway station and had been there for a few weeks when one morning, the village awoke to find them gone. They had, however left something behind, a puppy that they obviously had no place in their hearts or their lives for. The children found her on the other side of the fence that separated the field where they'd camped from the busy railway line. She was tied to a post and couldn't go far. The poor thing was actually on the railway line, where she could easily have been hit by a train and killed. What a callous way to abandon an unwanted puppy. Ignoring their own safety, the group of four children worked hard to undo the rope holding the puppy and then ventured on to the railway to lead the pup to safety. The children, Lisa told us, were no more than eleven or twelve years old and it was a very brave though foolhardy thing they did that day in saving the puppy from almost certain death. They then wondered what to do with puppy and one of them suggested they take it to 'the dog lady' who lived nearby. So, Lisa found herself with an extra mouth to feed until she could re-home the puppy, but had so far been unable to find a suitable home for the foundling.

What could we do? Neither of us was prepared to turn this happy little dog down. She needed a new home and Lisa knew she'd found the right people to adopt little 'Pancake' though Juliet did say to her that we would want to rename her. Somehow, she couldn't see herself on our local playing field calling 'Pancake' at the top of her voice when recalling the dog. I had to agree and Lisa didn't mind at all. All she cared about was finding a good home for the dog. A few minutes later, the dog was in our car and on her way to her new home. She seemed so pleased to be going with us and literally tried to leap into the back of our Mondeo Estate car, though her little short legs weren't long enough to allow her to make it. Juliet helped her up and she instantly settled down on the dog cushion we kept in there. As I drove the few miles to our home, Juliet and I discussed alternative names we could call her. Various names were suggested and discarded and then Juliet said, "Come on, we have to think of a good name for a dog who hasn't cost us a penny."

"There you are," I replied. "You've nailed it. Let's call her Penny."

So that was it. In that short conversation in the car, Pancake became Penny. Juliet kept looking back to see if our new doggie friend was behaving in the back. As she never saw her once during the journey we had to assume she was being a good dog, which was confirmed when we got home and opened the tailgate. The newly-named Penny was fast asleep. Talk about being laid back!

Our other dogs took to Penny from the first minute we brought her in to our home. She was as laid back with them as she had been in the car and Penny made herself at home in no time at all. Most of our dogs seemed to take no notice of the newcomer in their midst, though one little dog proved to be quite inquisitive about Penny. Who else could that have been but Cassie of course? She sniffed her, wagged her tail at her, tried touching noses with her, though Penny appeared none too sure about that part at first, but very soon, the two small dogs were acting like the best of friends.

I can truthfully say that I've never known a dog settle into a new home as quickly as Penny did. She behaved as if she'd been with us all her life. She soon joined my little gang on the field and even Cindy was quick to make friends with her. We did make two rather amusing observations about Penny. First, her legs. When she sat, her front legs had a slightly 'bowed' appearance and if you know anything about furniture, you'll know what I mean when I say she looked as though she had 'Queen Anne' legs. Second, due to her markings, with quite a lot of white fur mixed in with the black on her face, she did look rather older than she really was. We weren't the only ones to notice that feature, because whenever Juliet or I took Penny for her walks with some of the other dogs, our friends and general 'doggie' acquaintances would remark, with comments like, "Oh how nice. You've been and adopted a little older dog." Or, something like "Nice to see you taking in senior dogs as well, now. How old is she?"

People were amazed when we explained that Penny was only about eighteen months old. Now that she's over thirteen years old, she still looks pretty much as she did as a young dog, so perhaps we could say she's aged extremely well.

But, back to those early days, and Penny would usually accompany me in the morning, and used to love playing with the other dogs and really enjoyed playing with her ball, definitely her favourite toy. Cassie and Cindy would usually play together and every playtime would end up with the pair of them enjoying a game of 'nose tennis' while the rest of the gang on the field carried on playing around them.

Penny often came with me and 'my team' in the afternoon as well, but would sometimes go with Juliet and her dogs in the afternoon, to give her the opportunity to meet and play with other dogs too. She really was the most sociable and affable little dog. She got along with everyone, both dog and human. Cassie, in contrast, got along with those she chose to. She was, from the beginning of her life with us, very choosy about the dogs she was happy to play with or be around. If she was a human being, I guess we might think of her as being a bit 'snooty' and 'snobbish' as if she thinks she's better than everyone else and can afford to decide who she will or won't like. Maybe that has something to do with her being only twelve inches long and weighing not much more than 5 kilograms. I'm sure you've all heard the old saying about 'small dog, big attitude.'

That just about sums up 'the Cassie monster' or, as she was soon nicknamed by those of us who knew her best... *The Mad Ferret.*

Penny

Chapter 6

What's a Mad Ferret?

Now, I'm sure everyone knows what a ferret is, right? Described on various online sites as being, *the domesticated form of the European polecat, ferrets are lively, fast-moving, curious, fun-loving little animals with a very inquisitive nature.*

Does the above description remind you of anyone? Maybe a certain little canine of your recent acquaintance, perhaps? You might think I'm referring to Cassie, and of course you'd be quite correct. Allow me to explain.

When I took Cassie on the playing field there were lots of bushes and shrubs planted all-round the border of the field, and whenever Juliet took her on the other, larger field where she'd meet up with her other doggie friends, there were many small copses dotted all around the place. These of course provide any dog of an inquisitive nature with a fertile source of places to indulge their desire to get their noses to the ground and sniff around under the bushes and trees.

In Cassie's case, once allowed off the lead to run free and play, she'd make a bee-line for the bushes, or trees. This wouldn't have been so bad, except for the fact that once she'd disappeared into the bushes etc. it was virtually impossible to get her back. There has never been any question about Cassie's hearing which is, if anything, more acute and sensitive than any of our other dogs, so it was never a question of her not hearing whoever was calling her. Oh no, in her case it was simply a matter of 'selective deafness.' If Cassie had found something interesting under those trees or bushes she would steadfastly refuse to come back until she'd done whatever it was she felt she needed to do in there. Quite often she'd find someone else's lost tennis ball, or maybe a tug toy or something similar and would proudly, (eventually), come strutting back across the field with her new treasure in her mouth and her tail held high in celebration of a successful 'hunting' mission. She'd look so proud of herself, it was impossible not to smile at her antics and even though she may have been gone far longer than she should have done, we could never be angry with her. After all, the main purpose of those sessions on the fields was enjoyment and exercise, and Cassie was certainly getting more than her fair share of both. It was after one such session, when Juliet was telling me how she'd disappeared under the bushes one day and described her as 'ferreting around' in the undergrowth, that I turned to the little dog and said to her, "Cassie, you're nothing but a mad ferret." That was it. Juliet laughed, I laughed, and Cassie just stood there looking up at us with her little tail wagging like mad. The name stuck and we've used it as an alternative name for her ever since, so much that she will in fact respond if we simply call, "Ferret, where are you?" or similar. Even the single word, ferret, can bring her running to us from anywhere in the house.

Even though Cassie is now well into her senior years, she had never lost her inquisitive streak and very often, if Juliet stops to talk to a friend while out on the field with the dogs, (she usually takes Cassie with Digby and Honey), the dogs will carry on playing quite happily, or often just sit quietly at her side, but when she turns to go, Cassie will be nowhere to be found. Juliet doesn't worry too much as she knows that Cassie will be off 'ferreting' around in the bushes and trees around the field. Sure enough, if she continues her walk as normal, with Digby and Honey running along and playing, all of a sudden, a little grey streak will suddenly appear from under a bush or a thicket of trees and come running at top speed to catch up with everyone else, with what can only be described as a cheeky look on her face as if to say, "it's okay, I'm here, you can carry on now."

Cassie is so tiny and her tail looks so comical as she holds it up and curled slightly over her back that it's impossible to be angry with her for doing her disappearing act. After all, she's quite safe on the field, with nowhere else for her to go and there are always a few other dog owners out there exercising their dogs at the same time, so if she did appear to have gone missing, Juliet can easily call on a ready-made search party.

As we're talking about nicknames in this chapter, it's probably appropriate that I mention another of Cassie's well-earned alternative names. Have I mentioned previously that Cassie just loves playing with a ball? Of course I have, and it's her love of balls that went a long way towards her earning the name 'The Wicked Witch of the West', or just 'The Wicked Witch.' In Cassie's mind you see, a ball is a ball, is a ball, and what are balls made for? Right, for playing with. Trouble is, Cassie has difficulty in understanding that every ball she sees isn't actually HERS. I'm quite certain you can imagine the kind of problems this obsession of hers with all things round and bouncy might lead to. Yes, of course, I'm pretty sure you know what's coming next. Cassie is a ball thief, and no dog's ball, whether it be a Rottweiler, Doberman, or a West Highland Terrier, is safe when Cassie is around. So often she will confidently run up to the biggest of dogs, (her attitude can be classified as brave, bordering on foolhardy), and, usually much to the dog's, and the dog owner's surprise, she will jump up and literally steal a ball from the other dog's mouth and run like hell, ball in mouth, tail over her back with the owner left standing slack-jawed in shock and their dog pretty much in the same state. Just what the heck just hit them? I can imagine their thoughts as this tiny little thing, smaller than many people's cats, pulls off a perfect example of daylight doggie robbery!

Of course, it then falls to Juliet to try and catch Cassie and return the stolen ball to its rightful owner. It can be quite hilarious sometimes, watching Juliet, another lady or maybe a man, together with their dog, traipsing across the field in hot pursuit of Cassie, who by now would probably be happily running around with her stolen treasure in her mouth. We're convinced Cassie knows just what she's doing, and that she's in the wrong by taking the other dog's ball, but again, her diminutive size and the cheeky look on her face usually means that the aggrieved owner of the dog victim of Cassie's highway robbery will usually be highly amused at her antics and there is always much laughter involved. Retrieving the stolen ball isn't always a success and often the other owners will simply say, "Let her keep it," or "She's so cute. I haven't the heart to take it from her."

Now, before I hear a chorus of 'aw' or 'how sweet' and so on, let me tell you what happens when the roles are reversed, and some other dog tries, or worse still, succeeds, in stealing Cassie's ball.

One day, when Cassie was running around and playing on the field, with Juliet and a couple of the other dogs, they were joined by a friend and his dog, a rather large but very friendly Doberman called Max. Thinking it would be fun to join in with Cassie's game, Max waited until Cassie dropped her ball and he leapt in to take it in his mouth. Cassie instantly reacted by screeching her high pitched bark at Max, her tail held rigid and her face contorted into a vicious looking snarl, (as vicious at it's possible to appear when one looks like a cross between *Batfink* and a *Mogwai*, the little characters from *Gremlins*). While Juliet and Max's owner looked on in amusement, their laughter turned to shock as poor Max seemed stunned by Cassie's display of aggression, dropped the ball and ran away. Not only did he run, but Cassie took off like a bat out of hell in hot pursuit, as if she wanted to punish him for having the temerity to steal her ball. Try and picture the sight it must have made, the long legged Doberman running away with little Cassie, her legs going like tiny dynamos, chasing after him. Max's owner couldn't stop laughing, and Juliet found herself calling Cassie back, not that she would have done anything if she'd caught up with Max, it was just so funny to see. Eventually, Cassie came back and a few seconds later, a crestfallen Max returned to his owner, who was still highly amused by what had just happened. So much for his big, brave Doberman, he commented. Chased away by a dog no bigger than an average family cat!

I think you now get the picture. Cassie may be tiny, but she has the attitude of a wolf. One can certainly understand how our domestic dogs are descended from their wild ancestors if our *Mad Ferret* is anything to go by. Cassie's attitude soon earned her a comical reputation on the field among the doggie people. Max wasn't the last dog to feel her wrath either, as over the years, she's chased a collection of other dogs that thought taking her ball was a good idea. They all learned differently!

Mad ferret with ball

Chapter 7

Here Come the Staffies

By now, Cassie had established herself as an integral member of the pack and of our family. I must just relate one of her other little idiosyncrasies before going further however. I wonder if anyone else has a dog who has such an amusing way of having a wee! Cassie's tale certainly wouldn't be complete without a mention of this strange practice of hers.

When she needs to 'go' she has a very peculiar habit of stopping when she finds an appropriate place, usually next to a low-growing bush or plant. Then she rears up on her front legs, looking like she's doing a handstand, and with her back end in the air, she raises her tail out of the way and commences to do her wee. It's so funny to see and most people who witness her doing this can't help commenting on it and having a laugh at the same time.

Now, back to our tale. As I've previously mentioned, in the years since Cassie joined us, there have been numerous changes to the members of our pack. As this book is a happy story of Cassie's life with us, I won't be going into details about various events that led to us losing various beautiful members of our little pack as time went on. I'd rather concentrate on the events that influenced Cassie's life and the dogs concerned with them at the time.

Which brings me to what I'll refer to as 'The Staffy era.' One sunny weekend we decided to take a drive to the local dog pound, some 12 miles from our home. While there, my step-daughter, Rebecca was looking in the various dog pens and called me to look at one particular dog. I joined her and watched as a sleek black dog with a white flash on his chest was carefully pulling his blanket from his bed to the spot in his pen where the sunshine was concentrated. Having succeeded he proceeded to lie in his comfy sunny spot to enjoy the afternoon sun. I called Juliet across and we watched the dog for a few minutes and our initial thoughts were, *what an intelligent dog he is.* After a few minutes looking at the other dogs in the pound, all of whom were deserving of new, forever homes, we decided to make enquiries about the black dog Rebecca had found.

"Oh, you mean Dexter?" said the lady at the office.

"He's got a name already then?" I said, somewhat surprised. Most dogs at the pound are strays or street dogs and rarely have names.

"Yes," the pound lady replied. "We scanned him when he arrived and found he was microchipped. We contacted the registered owner who told us to keep him. They'd apparently given him away and didn't want him back. We were suspicious as the warden who brought him to us told us he'd been thrown from a moving car doing about 60 mph, on the motorway. He was seen bouncing onto the hard shoulder by another motorist who stopped to help him and who took him to a vet. He was lucky to escape with severe bruising and no internal injuries."

Dexter's story clinched it for us. We completed the paperwork and paid a deposit. He would be ours in seven days if he wasn't claimed by his owner, which of course was as likely as snow falling on Christmas day in Australia. He was described on the paperwork as a Staffy/Labrador though time has led us to believe there's no staffy in him. He's just a Labrador cross of unknown parentage. We were just a little concerned at the time though, because this was a time when Staffordshire Bull Terriers were receiving a lot of negative press coverage and we wondered what we were letting ourselves in for.

We needn't have worried. Once he joined us at home Dexter proved to be a real gentleman. In fact, we often thought of him as being so laid back, he was almost horizontal. From day one, he has preferred his bed to the great outdoors, and going for walks probably ranks at about number ten in his top ten favourite things to do! He truly loves his bed, bless his heart, which is probably after what happened to him the day he was thrown from the car and which has probably left some mental scars that will never desert him.

Having acquired what we thought was our first 'staffy' type and being pleasantly surprised at his gentleness and good nature, we decided we'd look out for another staffy the next time we went looking for a new rescue to adopt.

In fact, when we did get our first staffy it didn't happen quite as we would have expected. If you've already read my last book, *Sheba: From Hell to Happiness*, you'll know the story of how we came to adopt Sheba, but in case you haven't read her story, I'll explain how we found our first 'real' staffy by including the following extract from her life story.

One Cold Christmas Holiday...

It had been a very cold winter already, and we weren't yet into January. It was that week between Christmas and New Year, ten Christmases ago, when the world seems a strange, surreal place as we slowly recovered from the festivities of Christmas and lumbered almost sleepily towards the revelry of New Year's Eve. Whether by coincidence or design, I really can't remember, but on the 29th day of that very cold December, with snow that had fallen a couple of days too late to call it a white Christmas lying on the ground, and with nothing better planned for the day, my wife suggested a visit to our local dog pound. I'd earlier bought a very large box of chocolates as a gift for the staff at the pound, from where we'd adopted a number of our family of rescue dogs in the past. It seemed the least we could do to say a small 'thank you' to the girls who worked there, doing their best to try to make their often frightened and scarred residents feel as comfortable as possible, given the circumstances in which they had to work.

The accommodations at the pound weren't luxurious by any standards, but at least the dogs held there were sheltered, fed and watered, and safe from harm, and the owners of the pound operated a strict 'no kill' policy at that time. If a dog couldn't be rehomed in a reasonable period of time, they would often contact the specific breed rescue society who would collect the dog and take it to be rehomed through their own organisations.

So, wrapped up against the cold, my wife and I, accompanied by our two girls, aged seven and eight and both in junior school, piled into the car and set off on the fourteen mile journey to the pound with our present neatly wrapped and decorated with ribbon and bow. On arriving at the pound, we parked in an almost deserted car park. Obviously, with the post-Christmas sales in full flow, looking for a rescue dog to adopt was a pretty low priority for the majority of the local population.

The girls on duty were pleased to see us as always and expressed surprise and gratitude that we'd thought to visit them with a present. One of the girls, who we knew quite well after numerous visits to the pound, informed us that since Christmas Eve, they'd received over two hundred dogs into their care, a staggering number of innocent, unwanted souls. We found it hard to believe that so many people could heartlessly 'dispose' of family pets in this way. As we were told, although some of the dogs had been handed in by their owners for various reasons, the vast majority had simply been cast out by their owners, some having been found and handed in by members of the public, with most having been picked up and delivered to the pound by the dog warden service.

Though we hadn't gone there that day with the intention of adding to our family of rescue dogs, (at that time I think we had eleven in our home), we were encouraged by our friend Lisa to take a tour of the facility. She explained that due to the numbers received, they'd had to set up 'overflow' accommodation, using outbuildings and even part of the stables that formed part of the property. So, off we went, and within a minute of leaving reception we were being assaulted by dozens of pairs of pleading eyes and wagging tails, all virtually pleading to be taken out of their pens and given a new home. Some were less active than others, lethargic and often cowering towards the back of their pens, obvious victims of cruelty or some form of abuse. It's almost impossible to resist the appeal of some of those dogs and I'll never understand how some people can visit such establishments and leave empty-handed, saying they couldn't find one they liked.

Anyway, we continued our tour, and after leaving the regular kennel accommodation behind we entered the overspill areas, the barn and stable areas, where the staff had done a great job in erecting dozens of secure but temporary living areas. We could hardly bear the heart-breaking sights of so many dogs, abandoned and unwanted over the biggest holiday period of the year.

"It's not been much of a Christmas for these poor babies has it?" I said to my wife who nodded in agreement, a lump in her throat preventing her from making a proper reply. As we entered a small extension to the stable area we saw a small pen in the corner, set slightly apart from the others. We made our way to view the inhabitant of that lonely corner but were unprepared for the sight that greeted us as we looked into it. Having already viewed terriers of all descriptions, hounds of varying sizes and colours, and many cross breeds of indeterminate parentage both my wife and I caught our breath at what we now saw.

A heat lamp hung suspended from the ceiling, positioned directly above a small, shrivelled almost hairless dog, curled tightly in a foetal position, shivering or trembling, or perhaps both. A few wisps of fur led us to think she probably originally had either a dark brown or brindle coat, but we couldn't be sure.

Juliet grabbed my arm in shock, her gesture enough to convey her thoughts, much the same as mine: How could anyone let a dog get into such a state?

Juliet found her voice and spoke softly, trying her best not to scare the little dog, who also had numerous red sores and wheals on its body, an obvious case of serious abuse. Perhaps worst of all was the bright red ligature mark round its neck, looking sore and raw. In addition, we could see virtually every bone in the dog's body. We were staring at a living skeleton!

"Hello baby," Juliet said. "Who could have done this to you?"

The dog didn't look up, and continued to lie in its bed, curled up under the warmth of the lamp. The girls at the pound had obviously done all they could to make the dog comfortable with a bed lined with extra blankets for warmth.

"It's bloody criminal," I said, my anger at the dog's treatment for a few seconds overriding my sympathy for its plight.

We were unable to stop our girls from peering into the pen and though they tried not to cry, I could see tears forming in their eyes as they took in the sight of this poor dog.

"Can you tell what breed it is?" Juliet asked me, quietly.

"I'm not sure. It's hard to tell, but at a guess, I'd say it's a little staffy," I replied.

"It looks close to death's door," my wife said, choking back her own tears at this terrible sight, this symbol of man's inhumanity towards an innocent living creature. "I want to ask Lisa about it."

I nodded in agreement. The girls volunteered to stay with the dog to 'keep it company' as Juliet and I made our way back to the reception office.

Lisa smiled as we walked back into the warmth of reception. "Bet you've found something you like, haven't you?" she said with a knowing look in her eyes.

"Maybe," Juliet replied. "What can you tell us about the little dog in the stables, the one under the heat lamp?"

"Oh, that one. She's a little Staffy. One of the wardens brought her in three weeks ago. If you think she looks bad now, you should have seen her then. She was in a hell of a state. We honestly thought she wouldn't make it and the vet wanted to put her to sleep, but she lifted her head and looked up at us and... well, something made us decide to do what we could to try and save her. It was coming up to Christmas after all. So, the vet did what he could to treat her injuries and her skin condition and though she's made some progress, I don't think she'll make it in the long run."

"But what on earth happened to her?" I asked.

"That's quite a story too. Seems the warden's office received an anonymous phone call one day, telling them a dog had been thrown on a rubbish tip, I can't tell you where, and that the caller thought it might still be alive. A dog warden went and found the dog, exactly as the caller described, and loaded her into her van and brought her here. Both the warden and the vet realised right away the dog had been badly abused. The lack of fur on her body indicates she's been used as bait to train fighting dogs. They shave the poor dogs, to make it easier for the fighters to grab hold of their skin."

This was actually the first time either Juliet or I had learned anything about the world of dog fighting and I'm sure our faces must both have reflected the horror we felt at what we were being told. After a pause for breath, Lisa continued her narrative.

"Our vet has been treating her since she arrived but there's not a lot more we can do. Her wounds are healing, but very slowly because of her poor overall condition. She's clearly been starved and the ligature marks round her neck are so deep it's obvious she's spent her life tied up while the fighters were trained to attack her. Poor dog has had no real life at all. From her size, we're guessing she was bred for fighting but turned out to be an undersized runt so they used her as a bait dog instead."

"So, what's going to happen to her?" I asked, knowing full well what was in Juliet's mind.

"The vet thinks she's so weak, it's unlikely she'll live long," Lisa replied. "Funny thing is, when she does lift her head and look up at you, she does her best to wag her tail and be friendly. Like every dog we see, she's looking for a little bit of love."

"It's just awful that people do things like that and get away with it," Juliet commented.

"Not awful, just plain criminal," I said.

Lisa seemed to be thinking for a minute before she said, much to our surprise.

"Look, we know how you feel about dogs, and you've already got a houseful at home, but… " she paused.

"But what?" I asked.

"Well...maybe, if the boss agrees, and if you're willing, you could maybe take her home and try and give her the love she needs for however long she's got left."

"Please, go and ask her," Juliet said. "We'll take her, no problem."

Lisa disappeared and returned two minutes later with Kay, owner of the kennels, who confirmed the offer Lisa had made to us.

Lisa led us back to the stable where the girls were still patiently waiting for us, talking gently to the little dog. Lisa opened the gate and walked in to the pen, bent down and began stroking the dog, who lifted her head up and, sure enough, her tail began to wag, slowly at first, then with a little more gusto when Lisa picked her up and passed her into Juliet's arms. Juliet immediately began talking softly to our new and unexpected rescuedog, and Lisa reached down and took a blanket from the dog's bed and wrapped it around the little waif to help protect her from the cold as walked across the yard to the office.

At reception, I was ready to fill out the necessary adoption papers and pay the usual fee for the dog but Kay held up her hand and told me they didn't want a penny for her.

"She's not exactly what people usually leave here with and she probably won't live very long. You two are marvellous for wanting to take her on and give her some loving care and affection. I doubt she's had one day of loving care in her life. Just take her home and do what you can for her. We'll do the basic adoption papers to comply with the legalities, but there'll be no fee for this little girl. You're doing us a favour by taking her."

A few minutes later, paperwork complete, and wrapped in a blanket we kept in the car at all times for our dogs, I carried our new rescue carefully in my arms and we gently loaded the little dog into our car, talking softly and reassuringly to her as we laid her on the large dog cushion that filled the large storage area in the rear of the estate car. As I closed the tailgate she looked at me and something seemed to spark in her mind and her tail wagged, just a little, as if she knew she was being rescued and going to a new home.

I drove slowly on the journey home, and the girls, who were quite small and could just see over the back seat, through the dog grille, reported that the little girl was sitting up and seemed far more alert and animated than she's appeared in the pound. As we headed for home, we held a discussion about a name for the latest addition to our rescue family.

"Poor thing deserves a really good name, something proud and noble," I said. "Something to make up for the bad times she's suffered."

"I agree," Juliet concurred and between us we reeled off various names that might be appropriate for her, with numerous suggestions coming from the girls in the back seat.

Nearing home, I'm not sure after all this time whether it was me or Juliet who thought of it, but one of us suggested the name 'Sheba' as in the Queen of Sheba, reputed to have been one of the most beautiful women of her time, and usually known simply as 'Sheba' and even though the children were too young to understand the significance of the name they agreed it was a nice name for the little dog. We quickly agreed it would be a great name for her, so as we pulled up outside our home the decision had been made. Henceforth, the poor bedraggled and mightily abused, almost hairless little Staffy would be known as Sheba!

Above extract from Sheba: From Hell to Happiness

So, we had ourselves a staffy, a real full pedigree Staffordshire Bull Terrier, not that she looked much like one at first. It took a lot of love and a lot of care before Sheba began to look a true staffy but within weeks of her arriving in our home she began to grow a lovely brindle-coloured coat and her scars and previous sores and ligature marks slowly disappeared beneath her newly grown fur.

As for Cassie, she took the arrivals of both Dexter and Sheba in her stride, as we'd expected her to. Nothing seemed to upset our little Cassie, and all she seemed to ask of any new arrivals was *"Do they like to play?"*

In Dexter's case, she quickly learned that he really wasn't very interested in playing, certainly not the way Cassie liked to play. Dexter was quite sedate on his walks, despite only being around 18 months old, running was something he gave the impression of looking down on. He'd join my little group on the playing field but rather than join in with the others, he was content to 'mooch' around the perimeter of the field, sniffing and snuffling in the shrubs and bushes that grew all around the borders. Occasionally, I'd find a discarded stick, and throw it in the hope he might find it interesting. He did, much to my surprise and he'd happily spend a few minutes chasing and bringing the stick back, until he decided he'd expended enough energy for the day and would suddenly ignore the stick and return to his exploration of the undergrowth.

Though Cassie had no problems accepting the new members of the pack, things weren't quite as simple from Sheba's point of view. Because she'd been used as a bait dog by the dog fighters, she came to us with an inherent fear of other dogs. While we were doing great, slowly getting her to accept the fact that the other dogs in the pack were not going to attack or hurt her, we eventually realised that she seemed to have a problem with Cassie. We deduced that it had to be because Cassie was such a live- wire, always bouncing around and jumping up and down, that she made Sheba very nervous. We didn't realise at the time just what the consequences of that nervousness would be.

Once again, I will include a short extract from *Sheba: From Hell to Happiness* to tell the story of what happened, and how it almost led to us losing Sheba for good.

Goodbye Sheba

It began as a normal Sunday. We all got up at the usual time, the dogs all enjoyed their usual breakfast and as we took them for their usual morning walks, none of us could have envisaged the trauma that lay in wait for us just a few short hours away.

The other dogs had all had a great time running free on the nearby playing field, and Sheba had enjoyed her longest lead walk to date.

Lunchtime came and went and, as was our usual routine on a Sunday afternoon, which we'd suspended for the three weeks Sheba had been with us, we decided to take a short trip to a nearby pub-restaurant, where children were allowed to accompany their parents. Juliet and I enjoyed this short break as a rule, being able to relax with a drink or two while the children could have a drink with us and run around and play in the gardens if they wanted to.

I found myself short of cash, so left everyone at home while I took a short trip in the car to the nearest ATM where I drew out some money for our Sunday afternoon trip out. As I pulled up outside our home, no more than ten minutes later, I still had no inkling of what was about to transpire.

All that changed as I walked through the back door to find Juliet in tears, cradling little Cassie in her arms, blood dripping from a wound, or wounds somewhere in the region of her front legs and shoulders. Not only was Cassie bleeding profusely but there was blood on the walls and carpet in the utility room. In fact, the utility room resembled a murder scene from a horror movie.

"What the hell's happened?" I blurted out, shocked by the sight that greeted me.

"It was Sheba," Juliet replied. "There was no warning. Everything was peaceful and she must have suddenly decided to attack Cassie for no reason. Look at the state of her."

I had to admit, Cassie looked terrible. Being a Yorkshire Terrier/Australian Terrier crossbreed, she was the smallest dog in the pack, not more than twelve inches long and weighing around four and a half kilograms, little more than two bags of sugar. With blood dripping from her wounds, and her coat matted and tangled with the blood that had already soaked her fur, it was hard to tell just how bad her injuries were.

"Something must have triggered it," I replied.

"But what?" Juliet cried. "As far as I know, Cassie did nothing to provoke Sheba."

"Where is Sheba now?"

"In the lounge. I managed to get her to let go and I just grabbed her collar and dragged her in there, out of the way," Juliet sobbed. "We can't keep her if she's going to start attacking the other dogs, Brian, she'll have to go back to the Pound, I'm sorry."

Much as I baulked at the prospect of returning her to the Dog Pound, Juliet's logic seemed sound at that moment.

"Where were the kids when it happened?" I asked as I tried to rationalise what had happened in those few sort minutes I'd been away from home.

"Thankfully they were upstairs in their rooms, but they both came running downstairs when they heard all the commotion and Cassie squealing. They're in the lounge with Sheba now. Sheba seems just as traumatised as Cassie, to be honest."

I could think of no way out of the situation at that point, other than Juliet's assertion that we had to return Sheba to the Dog Pound.

"Maybe she'd be better off in a home with no other dogs," I said as I looked at Cassie, my heart heavy with sadness for her injuries and also for Sheba, for whom we'd had such hopes. After all, she was still recovering from the abuse and neglect she'd suffered and had been doing so well. It did make sense at that time, to let her go and maybe they could find her another home with a family that would love her and give her their undivided attention.

Without saying another word, but with a heavy heart, I pulled my mobile phone from my pocket and reluctantly dialled the number for the Pound. I was grateful to hear the friendly voice of Lisa when my call was answered.

"Lisa, we have a problem," I said, in an unwitting parody of the words associated with the ill-fated Apollo 13 moon mission.

"What's wrong, can we help?" Lisa replied, obviously able to tell from the tone of my voice that something was seriously wrong.

She listened sympathetically as I explained what had happened and I almost choked on the words as I finished by saying, "Can I bring her back to you? Juliet says we can't trust her and if she does something like this again she could kill one of our dogs if we're not around to stop her."

"Of course you can," Lisa said. "Don't worry. It's not your fault. I'm sure you've done all you can for her."

"Thanks Lisa. I'll be there within the hour," I said and hung up and turned to Juliet. "I'd better get going then. You can go and see to Cassie while I'm out and if it looks bad after you've cleaned her up, I'll have to take her to the emergency vet."

"Yes, okay, I'll take her up to the bathroom when you've gone. I'll be able to see better when I've used the shower to get rid of most of the blood."

I walked through to the lounge to find Sheba sitting peacefully in between Victoria's feet. She got up as soon as I entered the room and walked to me, her tail wagging. I felt awful, and in fact, I could virtually feel my heart beating in my chest at the thought of taking her away from the only home she'd ever known, but it had to be done.

"You've been a very naughty girl, Sheba," I scolded her and her tail fell as if she could tell I was angry with her. "I'm taking her back to the Pound girls. Your Mum and I can't risk her doing something like this again."

Both girls looked really upset and Victoria asked if she could come with me to say goodbye to Sheba. I agreed, feeling that her company would be more than welcome on what I knew would be a rather lonely journey home.

When I clipped her lead on, Sheba again wagged her tail, thinking she would be going for a walk, but the walk extended no further than the car, where I picked her up and loaded her into the rear compartment of our estate car. I'd remembered to pick up her medications before leaving the house, hoping the people at the Pound would make sure she took her medicine and that they'd apply the gel to her still healing tail.

When we arrived at the Pound, Lisa was ready and waiting for us.

"What will happen to her now, Lisa," I asked.

"We'll do our best to rehome her, of course," she replied.

"She needs her tablets and her gel for her tail," I said. "Do you think you'll be able to give her her meds and see to her tail?"

"We will if we have time. You know how busy things can get round here."

"I know," I said feeling worse and worse by the second. If I was going to leave Sheba there, I had to go, as fast as I could.

When Lisa removed Sheba's collar and lead and placed a rope lead round her neck, I felt terrible. Poor Sheba dutifully walked away by her side until they reached the corner of one of the buildings that would take her out of sight. I looked round and Sheba was standing there, looking at me with pleading eyes that seemed to be saying, "Why are you leaving me here? What have I done? Don't you know I love you?"

Before I knew it, Lisa gave a little tug on her lead, and Sheba disappeared from our sight. I felt Victoria's hand suddenly take hold of mine and looked down and saw tears in her eyes. It took all my self-control not to join her in crying right there in the car park.

As we drove home in relative silence, I looked in my rear-view mirror and couldn't help seeing little seven-year old Victoria quietly sobbing on the back seat.

"Are you alright, Victoria?" I asked, already knowing the answer, but not knowing what else to say.

"I'm going to miss Sheba," she sniffed in reply.

"I am too, sweetheart," I replied, "but you do understand why we had to take her back, don't you?"

"Yes, I know, but couldn't we have given her one more chance?"

"Perhaps, but what if she did it again and maybe ripped poor Cassie to pieces? You wouldn't want that to happen, would you?"

"No," was the one-word answer that told me Victoria wasn't totally convinced by my argument, and, truth be told, neither was I.

"Don't forget, we might have to take poor Cassie to the emergency vet when we get home. It looked like her leg or her shoulder was badly hurt before we came out. We'll see how it looks after Mum's cleaned it up and had a good look at the wounds.

Victoria had fallen into silence and stayed that way for the remainder of our journey. We were soon home again and hurried into the house to see how Cassie was.

Juliet was waiting at the back door as we walked in, with Cassie in her arms.

"What's the verdict?" I asked her.

"Well, it's amazing really. She's not half as bad as I first thought. It obviously looked much worse than it really was. When I cleaned her up in the shower and had a really good look at the wound, it's not very big at all." She gently held Cassie's leg up to show me. There was a small bite mark in what we might term her 'armpit' where her leg joined her body at the shoulder. It was still bleeding a little bit but Juliet was mopping it up with a wet-wipe from time to time, to stop it dripping on the floor.

Juliet then looked at me and then at Victoria. She knew instantly that we were upset.

"What was it like when you took her back?" she asked.

"Awful, to be honest," I replied. "Sheba toddled off with Lisa but when she realised we weren't going with her she just stood still, staring at us, looking lost and alone. I felt like a mass murderer if you must know and Victoria was in tears, saying how much she'll miss her."

"Do you think she'll be okay?"

"I don't know. I don't even know for sure if they'll keep up with her medications."

"Well, at least Cassie looks as if she's going to be okay."

"She probably just needs some antibiotics to prevent infection. I'll take her to the vet tomorrow."

Suddenly, we fell silent, as though neither of us knew what to do or say. We'd never faced a situation like this before and I'm sure we both wondered if we'd done the right thing. Obviously, Cassie's screams and the amount of blood she'd lost initially had given us a slightly inflated view of her injuries, but we'd acted with the best of intentions, and we'd have to live with our decision.

"Why don't we go to the pub as we planned?" Juliet eventually broke the silence. "It will do us good to get out of her, have a drink or two and then come home and walk the dogs."

"What about Cassie?"

"She'll be okay. She probably just needs to lie down and rest anyway."

"Okay," I agreed, and we all went upstairs to get changed for our now slightly delayed visit to the pub.

Half an hour later, we set off, all four of us still in a rather subdued state. What had begun as a normal everyday kind of day had turned into a pretty awful one and though it had never crossed our mind until a couple of hours ago, the decision had been made. Sheba was gone!

Wrong Choices

The pub was warm, welcoming and filled with the usual hubbub that went with a crowded room populated by late Sunday dinner eaters, enjoying meals from the carvery, and an assortment of regulars and occasional visitors. The usual, middle-of-the-road piped music played at a comfortable volume in the background. I acted almost like an automaton at the bar, ordering my usual pint of Guinness, a white wine for Juliet and soft drinks and crisps for the kids. Somehow, being there didn't feel as relaxing and as good as it normally would have done.

As I sat at the table that Juliet and the girls had managed to secure for us, I was greeted by virtual silence apart from mumbled thanks. We sort of all sat staring into space for a minute or two before I broke the accompanying silence.

"I take it everyone's missing Sheba?"

"We are," Juliet replied. "I'm wondering if we were a little hasty in getting rid of her. We've been sitting here worrying about what might happen to her if they can't find anyone to adopt her. Plus, even if they do, will she get the care and attention she needs to recover properly and live a full and happy life?"

"I agree with everything you just said, but what can we do about it now. I've already taken her back and signed her over. And what about what she did to Cassie?"

"Maybe she just needs some special training. You could have a word with Brian Gallagher and see if he can suggest any ideas."

Brian was a canine behaviourist and trainer I'd worked with on some of our other dogs in the past and I knew if anyone could sort out any socialisation problems, he was the man.

"Maybe we should have discussed it more before rushing to take her back to the Pound," I said.

"It was my fault," Juliet said. "I just saw all the blood where she bit Cassie and thought it was far more serious than it really was. I should have waited until I'd cleaned her up before telling you to get rid of Sheba."

The children were sitting like statues as they listened to our conversation, until Victoria said, "Can't we get her back?"

Juliet added, "Yes, why don't you phone Lisa and see if they'll let us change our mind?"

I knew then that we all agreed. Returning Sheba to the Pound had been a very bad choice, not just for Sheba, but for the family too.

"I can try," I said, and without another word, I rose from the table, my Guinness still untouched, and walked outside, where I could make a phone call in peace.

"Lisa, it's me again," I said when her familiar voice answered my call. "We've had a family meeting, and we think we acted far too hastily in taking Sheba back to you. She deserves a second chance and if you don't mind, we'd like to give her that chance."

"Of course we don't mind," she replied.

"Thank God," I said. "I'm not sure how Juliet and the girls would have felt if you said no."

"We know you well enough by now," Lisa responded. "If you're willing to take her back, we know you'll do the best you can for her. We could all see what a difference the last few weeks with you have made to her since she was brought in to us originally."

"Thank you so much, Lisa. How soon can I come and get her?"

"It'll have to be tomorrow, I'm afraid. We're closing in about five minutes. There's no way you'll make it here by then, is there?"

"No, there isn't," I reluctantly agreed. "But I can be there as soon as you open at noon tomorrow."

Feeling greatly relieved, I walked back into the pub and quickly sat down opposite Juliet, reaching across and taking her hand in mine. The two girls sat waiting, expectantly.

"Well?" Juliet asked. "What did they say? Did you speak to Lisa, or was it Kay?"

"It was Lisa. She says it's okay for us to go and collect her tomorrow."

"That's such a relief," my wife replied and the two girls, Rebecca and Victoria both bounced up and down on their seats with excitement.

"Can't we get her back today?" Victoria asked.

"I'm sorry, but no, Victoria. The Pound closes any time now and we'd never get there in time. Don't worry, she'll be fine. It's only one night and then she'll be home with us again."

"But she'll be missing us, and her nice warm cosy bed, and her tea, and lying in the lounge with us all watching telly, and it's cold and horrible there," Victoria went on, making me feel even guiltier.

"I know she will, Victoria, but I'm sure she'll be okay and just think how excited she'll be when I turn up tomorrow to bring her home."

"What time are you picking her up?" Juliet asked.

"I'll be there when they open at noon," I replied. "Now that we've got it sorted, can we all try and cheer up a little and enjoy our drinks?"

Juliet squeezed me hand as she said, "Thank you," and I squeezed back. We knew we'd made a bad mistake and now we hoped we could correct it without it having had too much of a detrimental effect on Sasha.

"I'm also going to call Brian and make sure he's okay with me taking Sheba to a few training sessions," I said, referring to our friend the dog trainer.

"I still wish I knew what made her turn on Cassie like that," Juliet mused, trying her best to figure out just what had happened to cause such upheaval in the house just a short time ago.

"What were they doing at the time? Don't you remember?" I asked.

"Everything was the same as usual," Juliet replied. "The dogs weren't doing anything out of the ordinary, in fact, most of them were lounging in their beds when it all kicked off."

I could sense she was thinking of something and encouraged her to tell me what had sprung to mind. It could be important.

"Well, you know how Cassie loves to play?"

I nodded.

"What if she jumped on Sheba, trying to get her to play and her claws caught one of Sheba's sores or something like that? That would have been painful and Sheba's mind would have seen it as an attack, like when she was used as a bait dog."

"That would be typical, of Cassie," I replied. "That's probably what happened, though we'll never know for sure. We're just going to have to be extra vigilant until we know Sheba can be trusted not to do anything like it again. Brian will help to get her properly socialised."

When I made that particular statement, I was again forgetting the vast amount of abuse and trauma Sheba had been subjected to in her life so far. It was another minor error on my part, an assumption that we'd learn from in due course.

With the phone call made, arrangements in place to collect Sheba the following day, the atmosphere at our table lifted from one of gloom and despondency to one of hope and expectation. Whatever happened from that point onwards, Juliet and I knew we'd never let Sheba go again. Whatever it took, we were determined to make her life with us a happy one, and one in which she could become an integral part of our pack of rescue dogs. She'd done great up until that Sunday. There was no reason why she couldn't do even better once we brought her home again.

The girls were happy and talkative once more, and we all returned home from the pub to find Cassie full of live and vitality. The wound on her leg already looked so much better than it had when we'd left for the pub earlier. I said I'd still take her to the vet in the morning, just to be on the safe side, but I didn't think there was even need of any stitches to close the wound.

The rest of our dogs all seemed to realise there'd been trauma in the home and it was a relief to get them all taken out for their evening walks so they could release any built-up tension by running around and playing on the field near our home. Tilly, however, seemed rather subdued. She, more than any of the dogs, was clearly missing Sheba, her new friend.

"Don't worry, Tills," I said, using my nickname for her, "Sheba's coming home tomorrow."

I always used to tell people that I was certain Tilly could understand English. Whether she truly could or not, I don't know, but I can say that after I said those words, Tilly began furiously wagging her tail. She, too, was happy at the news!

Daddeeee!!!

The following morning dawned, bright and sunny, reflecting the overall mood in the house. Though we'd all missed Sheba the previous night, the feeling was tempered by the knowledge that I'd be collecting her and bringing her home again today.

First of all, however, I had to make a call to the vet to have Cassie's wound checked over. After we'd completed our early morning dog walks, I was in time to call the vets just after opening time. I had no trouble getting Cassie booked in and was given an appointment in just half an hour.

This time, instead of Bernard, I saw Rebecca, the practice manager, who at a future date would of course become Sasha's vet, as those who've read her story will know. Cassie bounded in to the surgery, full of her usual unbridled energy and I almost felt a fraud for taking her in. With all the really sick dogs who must be in need of attention, here I was with this bundle of boundless joy who looked as fit as a fiddle. Outwardly, there was no sign of her wound and the way she kept leaping from the floor up on to my lap and down and up again made her look like a demented Jack-in-the-box!

Rebecca soon called us in though, much to my relief and I quickly gave her a run down on the previous day's events, leaving out the fact we'd taken Sheba back to the Pound. She'd be with us again shortly, so her status bore no relevance to Cassie's immediate treatment. Rebecca agreed that the wound wasn't serious, though it took her a while to get Cassie to stay still long enough for her to examine it. No stitches were required and Rebecca gave her an injection of antibiotics and prescribed a few days on Metacam as a painkiller. She laughed when I said to her, "Does she look in pain to you, Rebecca?"

"Not really," she smiled, "but we'd better be on the safe side. It might feel a little stiff in a day or so, so the Metacam will help her cope with any discomfort."

I took the opportunity to ask Rebecca if she thought Sheba's bite on Cassie could have been a fear reaction, and after I'd given her a quick resumé of Sheba's history, she agreed that my theory was probably correct.

"If Cassie was leaping around and jumping on her the way she's bouncing around in here this morning, it wouldn't surprise me at all if Sheba felt threatened and tried to defend herself," she said.

"We'll try and make sure Cassie doesn't get the chance to do it again until Sheba's fully socialised with the rest of the dogs," I told her.

"That's a good idea, Mr. Porter. We wouldn't want any harm coming to either of them. From what you've told me, Sheba still has some healing to do. Bernard's taking care of her, isn't he?"

"Yes, he is, and Sheba's coming along really well."

"Good. So, this little one is fine and can go home. No need to bring her back unless you have any concerns. The wound should heal up in about a week to ten days. I know your wife was probably a little panicked by the bleeding you describe but remember that dogs tend to bleed very profusely in comparison to humans."

"Thanks, I'll remember that in future."

With that, I left the surgery, Cassie bouncing along beside me and a bottle of Metacam in my pocket. The first stage of today's busy schedule was completed.

Juliet was relieved when we got home, and I told her what Rebecca had said. We'd learned another lesson that morning and in future we'd remember that point about dogs bleeding rather more profusely than we do. It was information that over the years has stood us in good stead and prevented more than one unnecessary journey to the vets when a couple of our pets have sustained minor cuts and scratches. We already had the powder that helped to stop bleeding and we'd always use it whenever one our dogs sustained such injuries. Almost without fail, the bleeding would soon cease and after cleaning up any wounds, we'd usually find them to be not worth troubling the vet with.

Next job that morning was to phone Brian, the dog trainer. After giving him the details about Sheba and the incident with Cassie, he told me she'd be welcome at his classes and told me she could start on Saturday. Brian was unfazed by the incident with Cassie and as usual, was confident in his ability to correct Sheba's possible psychological problem in believing other dogs were going to attack her.

* * *

The morning flew by and before I knew it, the time had come for me to set off for the Dog Pound. Juliet asked if I wanted a bit to eat before leaving home, but I said I'd wait until I returned home with Sheba. The journey to the Pound normally took between 20 and 30 minutes, depending on the level of traffic, so I set off at 11.30, intending to be there just as they opened at noon.

My timing was perfect, and I pulled up in the car park at a couple minutes to twelve. The gates were still locked when I tried them but within a minute, Lisa arrived to open up.

"I take it you couldn't wait to get here," she laughed.

"You could say that," I replied. "How is she?"

"She's fine, don't worry. Once she sees you she'll probably just think she's been on a little overnight holiday. Let's go and do the paperwork again and then I'll go and get her for you."

"I'm sorry for messing you around, Lisa," I apologised.

"Listen you did what you thought was the right thing, and it's great you want to give her a second chance too, so don't apologise. I wish everyone who came here looking for a dog was as responsible as you and Juliet."

With that, we entered the office where the basic paperwork signing Sheba back over to us took only a minute. While Lisa went to fetch Sheba, I took her collar and lead from my pocket and waited at the same corner from which I'd walked away from her the previous day. A minute later, Lisa appeared at the corner of the building with Sheba walking submissively by her side. Lisa slipped the rope lead from around her neck and mouthed the words "Call her."

"Sheba, come here," was all I said and Sheba looked up, saw me standing waiting for her, and literally set off at full speed in my direction and ended her run with a leap in the air that took her into my arms. Thankfully, I caught her and was then subjected to a plethora of doggie kisses as she displayed her sheer joy and happiness at seeing me again.

Lisa was laughing and said, "I think that was her way of saying Daddeeeee. I think she's happy her Daddy's come back for her."

"I think you're right, Lisa," I laughed as well as I gently lowered Sheba to the ground where she stood wagging her tail with excitement.

"That's one of the nicest things I've ever seen," Lisa said. "That little dog obviously loves you so much and she's only been with you a few weeks."

"I know, that's what we worked out yesterday after I'd brought her back."

"I'm happy for her," Lisa replied as I walked towards her and shook her hand and said my thanks before turning and walking Sheba out of the gates, and soon had her settled in the car, after she'd actually tried to jump into the rear compartment. Sheba was going home... again!

I drove as fast as the speed limit would allow, keeping an eye on my rear view mirror, where I could see that Sheba was standing up, her paws resting on the bars of the dog grille, her head moving around as she took in the sights of the journey. Did she know where she was going? I'd like to think she did, and soon enough I pulled up outside our house, and as I exited the car, Juliet came walking down the path to meet us, having been watching for our arrival from the lounge window.

"Is she okay?" she asked, as I walked to the rear of the car to open the tailgate.

"See for yourself," I replied, lifting the tailgate, allowing a hugely excited little Staffy to leap from the car onto the road, jumping up and down, her front paws wrapping themselves around Juliet's legs in a loving grip, her tail wagging furiously.

"Sheba, hello again. Wow, anyone would think you'd been gone for a year. You're home now, baby," Juliet exclaimed as she tried to calm Sheba's delight and exuberance.

"You should have seen what she did at the Pound," I said, and went on to explain to Juliet about Sheba's leap into my arms when she saw me.

"Come on then, let's get you inside," Juliet said as we led Sheba down the path towards the back door. She'd deliberately left Tilly and a couple of the other dogs in the back garden so Sheba could be greeted by familiar faces as we walked through the gate. Sure enough, there was a great deal of tail wagging and sniffing each other as Sheba quickly became reunited with her doggy pals.

"It's going to be interesting to see how Cassie acts when she sees her," I said.

"Only one way to find out," Juliet said as she opened the back door and called the other dogs out into the garden.

They all came running out, some stopped to see Sheba, most just ran down the garden and carried on as if she wasn't there, including Cassie, who didn't seem to have any fear or trepidation when she realised Sheba was back. In fact, over the years, we've found Cassie to be one of the toughest and most dominant of our dogs, despite her miniscule size.

As our pack has developed over the years, we've realised that the other dogs are actually quite scared of little Cassie. I mention this in case anyone thinks Cassie is a tiny, 'victim in waiting', surrounded by bigger dogs just waiting to take chunks out of her. Not for nothing do we call her 'The Mad Ferret' or 'The Wicked Witch of the West'. She's like a Duracell Bunny without an off switch, and even now, at the age of twelve, she can run and run and run all day with no sign of fatigue. It can make you tired just watching her.

She also loves to hide under the coffee table in the lounge in the evening, or alternatively will 'perch' on the back of the sofa, from where she has a great position to survey the rest of the room. If any dog tries to disturb her while under the table, she'll leap out at them like a Moray Eel striking from its undersea hiding place, letting out a high-pitched screech, (not a bark), and it's quite hilarious to see the Staffies, like Sheba, (really), Muttley and Sasha running into the centre of the room and rolling on the backs, legs in the air in submission, or often running out of the room altogether. Those who encroach on her space on the back of the sofa usually receive similar treatment. This tiny terrier, (should that be 'terrierist?') is definitely no shrinking violet.

Above extract from Sheba: From Hell to Happiness

Serious lessons had been learned by all of us and thanks to our subsequent careful management of the dogs activities no such incidents ever took place again. By the time you read this book, Cassie is 14 years old, Sheba we estimate to be 12 or 13, (the dog pound could only guess at her age when we adopted her), and the two of them live in peace for the most part, with Sheba still being quite afraid of the tiny 'Mad Ferret' and who keeps out of her way whenever she can! Cassie is definitely what we humans might best describe as a 'wind-up merchant.' The other dogs, and even those she meets while out running and playing, seem to know they need to give her a wide berth. She's got an attitude the size of the Empire State Building, which, taking into account her diminutive stature (in other words she's a shrimp), is quite understandable.

Walkies with Sasha & Sheba

Chapter 8

Peace

Time seemed to fly by as peace returned to our household. We had definitely learned our lesson from the Sheba incident and Juliet and I worked out what we thought was a better way of managing our family of rescues. Among other measures we introduced was a way of keeping Cassie a little safer by letting her spend most of the day in the lounge, instead of being in the kitchen with the other dogs. Until then, we had allowed them all to spend their time together, with the large kitchen giving on to the utility room where they also had free access and so to the back door where they could go out into the back garden whenever they wanted to .Our back garden is surrounded by a six foot high fence to make it safe and secure for the dogs. From that time Cassie would be closely supervised whenever we let her out to go into the garden. So that she wouldn't get too lonely in the lounge we allowed Penny to join her so she would have company during the day. In the evenings, we always allow the dogs to join us in the lounge so we were confident that she'd be ok with us both there to supervise things.

Strangely enough, Cassie and Sheba have been quite close ever since that incident, though Sheba always gives us the impression she is slightly afraid of the little 'mad ferret.'

Our doggie family was later added to when Sasha joined us. Abandoned in a gutter at 5/6 weeks old, this little staffy puppy soon had everyone falling in love with her. She'd been almost dead from hypothermia when found by a passing dog warden, and was so young we'd had to go out and buy puppy milk for her for the first couple of weeks after adopting her. Then, at ten weeks old, she broke her left front leg while playing with one of the other dogs, as she fell down the stairs and landed awkwardly. After an operation to repair the leg, she then had to spend three months in a crate while she recovered, only allowed out for toilet breaks and short periods of exercise. Eventually she got the all clear, and then just two weeks later, she tried to jump the baby gate in the kitchen and guess what... she landed badly and broke the same joint again! Another operation followed, and then another three months of crate recuperation. There would be no more broken limbs, but at around one year old she developed serious skin allergies, which we and her vet struggled to bring under control, Everything else would pale into insignificance however, when at two years old, Sasha came in from the garden one morning and suddenly collapsed in the utility room. We had no idea what was happening to her as her legs flailed around and she was drooling, lost control of her bladder and was making a horrible noise that came from deep in her throat. We thought she might be having a stroke and could do nothing to help her until she eventually came round from the seizure and we were able to give her lots of cuddles and love until the vet opened and I rushed her in as an emergency. That was the fateful day we discovered our baby girl had canine epilepsy, since when Sasha and our management of her illness have become part of our daily life routine.

You might be forgiven for thinking our original desire to own a staffy was a mistaken one, but I have to say we wouldn't have it any other way. Both Sasha and Sheba are the most loving, cuddly dogs imaginable and both are tremendously happy, and Sasha even has a Facebook page called Sasha, the Wagging Tail of England, which was started by an American friend of mine, Edward Cook, a great fan of Sasha's from all the photos and videos I used to post on my Facebook page about her. Since he opened it, the site has gained in popularity and now has almost 700 followers.

While all this drama was taking place in our home, Cassie just went about her daily life as if nothing was wrong, at least, nothing that concerned her. As long as she had a ball to play with, and her two daily runs to play on the field, she was happy and contented. Her daily playtimes with Cindy continued to be a source of joy and happiness for her and her little friend, and for me and Maureen, Cindy's human mum to witness. Indeed, the change in Cindy since she'd met Cassie and our other dogs was simply miraculous. She'd gone from being nervous, quivering jelly around other dogs, to being a happy, confident little dog who, as soon she appeared on the playing field, would be looking for us. If we were first there, Maureen would confidently let her off her lead and she'd run at full speed across the field to get to us, and where she and Cassie would go through their 'greeting ritual' of touching noses, wagging tails and running around in circles together for a few seconds before looking to me and Maureen to produce a ball so they could indulge in their favourite 'nose tennis' game.

Cindy was quite a bit older than Cassie, as the years passed she became less of a regular on the field. Age wasn't being particularly kind to Cassie's friend and she would often be missing from our playtimes on the playing field due to visits to the vet as she entered her senior years. As Victoria grew older, she also found other interests, as teenage girls do, and soon it became impossible for me to take four of five dogs at a time for their play sessions. Juliet instead took some of the dogs I usually walked on her walks to the other larger field in the village and I saw less and less of Maureen and Cindy.

One day, I was in the local supermarket and came across a tearful Maureen. Poor Cindy had been taken very ill and the vet advised Maureen that it would be the kindest thing to let her go, so Maureen had lost her companion of many years. It would be a couple of years before Maureen found another little dog, a Border Terrier named Millie, that once again brought her happiness, but the pain of loss returned sooner than she might have expected, as, after less than two years, her dog would be diagnosed with advanced diabetes, which poor Millie must have been suffering with long before Maureen adopted her, and sadly had to be put to sleep. I felt incredibly sad and sorry for Maureen who seemed lost without a dog to walk and feel close to and I would often bump into her husband, Zoran, as he went for a walk around the village, and he told me himself that Maureen just wasn't the same person without a dog. He would do all he could to find another dog they could take into their home, but Maureen was understandably reluctant to lay herself open to further heartbreak so soon.

Thankfully, she knew herself that she needed a dog around her, and one day, as I was walking Sasha and Sheba, who should I see coming towards me, but Maureen, walking her newly adopted dog, Ellie, a beautiful little terrier crossbreed, with a very fluffy, beautiful grey and white coat and an even fluffier tail. Apparently, Ellie is a Shih tzu/Yorkie Cross, but whatever she is, Maureen had regained her smile, and her purpose in life. I was so happy for her that day and I often see her walking Ellie around the village and Maureen still retains a great interest in my dogs, and she always stops to talk to them, as she's now known them for most of their lives with us.

I'm glad that for her, at last, there's been a happy ending and a new beginning after the loss of Cindy.

Chapter 9

Lost and Found

It's a certain fact that, to use and old cliché, time flies when you're having fun, and those words were never truer than when applied to Cassie. Before we knew it, our little 'Mad Ferret' was celebrating her tenth birthday and showed absolutely no signs of slowing down or acting as many ten-year-old dogs would. Oh no, quite the contrary. Cassie woke up every day with just two things in mind, running and playing. When I mention her birthday, we don't know the exact date she was born but we have always used the date that Linda first rescued her, and taken twelve weeks off that time to give us a rough approximation. After all, everyone needs a birthday, right?

So, older she may have been, but she continued to spend each day like a Duracell Bunny without an off switch. People, us included were simply astounded to witness her boundless energy and wondered where on earth it all came from. I used to joke that it must be the Australian in her. Maybe she's part kangaroo. Well, she can certainly jump around enough! There's never been a day when Cassie wasn't primed and ready to go from the moment we rose in the morning. The only time she really slowed down was after tea in the evenings, when we allow all the dogs to join us in the lounge until bed time. By the time Juliet and I have eaten our evening meal, the dogs are ready to relax, (thank God) and that means we can also take some time to put our feet up in front of the TV and 'switch off' for a couple of hours before we head upstairs to bed.

It has long been Cassie's routine, once we settle down, to jump up and join me on my armchair, where she quickly squeezes herself in between my leg and the chair arm, where she quickly goes into a nice, deep sleep, and yet, if any of the other dogs gets up to leave the room or if there's the slightest sound out in the street, the super-hearing of those bat-sized ears of hers comes into play and she instantly wakes up and goes into full alert mode. There's no escaping the ever-vigilant Cassie.

* * *

It was during the summer, soon after she'd reached ten years of age that Cassie performed what I like to call her 'Houdini act.' In other words, she disappeared! The afternoon walk was always Cassie's favourite time, when she could really stretch her legs and do her own thing. With lots of people and dogs around you'd think it would be difficult to lose a dog, but, it's as well to remember that Cassie has never been what we could really call a 'normal' dog.

It seemed no matter how hard or how closely Juliet tried to keep a close watch on her, Cassie had the speed, skill and determination to 'do her own thing' regardless of the supervision of us mere humans. It was easy to keep an eye on Digby and Muffin as they were happy to run and play with their other doggie friends and would invariably stay close to and within sight of Juliet.

So it was that on one particular day, with the sun shining brightly and butterflies in the air, Juliet stopped during her walk, as she often did to talk to her friends who had arrived as usual for their afternoon walks with their dogs. As usual, the dogs were running around, having fun, though because it was an unusually hot afternoon, Cassie seemed less inclined than usual to want to play ball or to exert herself too much. That was unusual enough in itself as under normal circumstances, Cassie would literally run and play until she was fit to drop and her little tongue would be hanging out from the side of her mouth like a piece of wet lettuce. Instead, she seemed content to wander around the field, investigating the shady spots in the copses and foraging under the bushes. Most of the dogs on the field that day were happy to stay close to their owners and stretch out enjoying a spot of basking in the warmth of the afternoon sun.

Juliet, as she always did, kept checking to make sure our three dogs on the field with her were okay, knowing that Cassie was happily 'ferreting' around, was happy enough seeing Digby and Muffin enjoying the sunshine together with our friends' dogs.

When it came to going home time for everybody, Juliet had no trouble gathering Digby and Muffin to her side; both of them responding instantly to her calls for them to join her. Of Cassie, however, there was no sign at all. Thinking she must still be exploring the trees and bushes, Juliet called her, and then called her some more, but received no response. Juliet wasn't too worried at this point, thinking that maybe Cassie was lying down, snoring her little head off, in a nice sunny spot in one of the copses, or perhaps she'd been too hot and had found a cool spot to lie down and have a nap.

Among the friends who's met up to walk their dogs together that day was a young man called Stuart, aged about twenty-two, and a student at Edinburgh University, who always came on the field, usually accompanied by his sister, Chloe to walk their family dog, Lenny, whenever he was home for the holidays. Stuart is intelligent, well-mannered and very different from some of the young men our country seems to be producing these days. I mention this only because he instantly realised that Juliet was becoming worried when, after about ten minutes of calling and searching, she'd failed to find Cassie. Stuart, knowing Juliet needed to take the other dogs home, as I'd be worrying about them, told her to come home, and he'd continue searching for Cassie. Juliet was so grateful to the young man who stepped up to help while other dog owners left Juliet to search by herself.

Juliet hurried home and quickly left Digby and Muffin with me after giving me a brief explanation of the situation. I was worried, to say the least. Cassie had never wandered off before, and the thought she might have been picked up and 'dognapped' by some unscrupulous person was never far from my mind as I waited for news. Knowing what often happens to such dogs, particularly as we had our former bait dog, Sheba, in the family, filled me with dread.

I lost track of time until eventually, Juliet arrived home, accompanied by Stuart, Chloe, Lenny…and Cassie! Stuart had insisted on walking Juliet home while he'd explained what had happened. We had to piece certain parts together, but a fairly clear picture appeared of Cassie's latest adventure.

Not far away from the playing field where we exercise the dogs, is a school, one with a very large playing field of their own. The school and its grounds are surrounded by a tall, green, diamond patterned fence, made from reinforced plastic, (you know the kind of thing I mean, it has steel running through it to give it added strength). It's designed to keep people and animals out as well as to ensure the safety of the children during the school day.

Well, after Juliet had left to bring Digby and Muffin home, Stuart explained that he'd done a quick search around our field once again, and then, applying some thought to the situation, he decided to look a little further afield. The path that leads from the field in the direction of the school gives way onto a narrow pathway that runs alongside the school playing field and leads to the next village. Stuart had wondered if Cassie might have found her way to the narrow path that resembled an alleyway, and found her way to the neighbouring village. As he walked along the path he suddenly noticed Cassie in the distance, running along quite happily on the school's playing field.

"Cassie," he called to her, and sure enough, she came running up to him almost immediately. The problem was, Stuart couldn't see how or where she'd found her way onto the school's property, and the fence was at least six feet high, so he had no way of getting to her, or getting her out, unless he could find out how she'd entered the field.

He walked up and down the length of the path, with Cassie bouncing around on the other side of the fence. Eventually, he came across a small break in the bottom of the fence, hardly noticeable unless someone had been looking for it. As far as Stuart could work out, this had to be the way Cassie had gained entry to the school grounds. Having found it however, he was faced with a new problem. How could he convince Cassie to first of all come to the gap in the fence, and secondly, convince her to squeeze back through the fence so he could rescue her and take her back to Juliet who he knew would be returning to continue searching for Cassie very soon?

Fortunately, Stuart had a few biscuits in his pocket, and Lenny, who Cassie normally ignored when they met, began scratching around at the bottom of the fence, having seen the little dog on the other side, which attracted Cassie to the right area.

Having attracted her to the general area, Stuart was then faced with the problem of enticing her through the small break in the fence, using the biscuits as a lure. He began by throwing a biscuit through the hole in order to get Cassie's attention. That ploy succeeded in as much as Cassie ran up and grabbed the biscuit, only to run off about ten yards with it, where she settled down on her tummy to eat it. "Oh dear," Stuart thought. "How on earth do I get her closer and show her how to get through the fence?" Cassie then took matters into her own paws by coming back to the fence, obviously looking for another biscuit. Stuart had a brainwave. He put his hand through the gap in the fence and placed a biscuit about six inches into the school side of the fence and proceeded to lay a small trail of biscuits from there to where he stood on the footpath side of the fence. As she gained in confidence, (and as her greed increased), Cassie gradually began devouring the biscuits, watched jealously, so Stuart told Juliet, by Lenny, as little Cassie ate up all his treats.

At last, as Stuart held his breath, Cassie's head appeared through the gap, not enough to grab her, but one more biscuit might do it. At last, her body followed her head and Stuart quickly swept her up in his arms and snapped her lead, that Juliet had left with him in case he found her, in place on her collar.

He placed her on the ground and began walking towards the exit from the field, just as Juliet reappeared after dropping Digby and Muffin off at home. She was so happy to see Cassie trotting along beside Stuart, with Lenny on the other side. She was also extremely grateful to Stuart for his help, and for volunteering to search for Cassie while she took the other dogs home. He even insisted on walking her home, to make sure she and Cassie got home safely. I was looking anxiously out of the window when I saw Juliet and Stuart appear, and though I couldn't see Cassie, who is too small to be seen through the garden wall, I could see Juliet was holding her lead so it was obvious that Cassie must be on the end of it.

I went out to meet them and was able to add my thanks to Stuart for his help and kindness in helping to find our little disappearing dog. He said he'd been happy to help and soon left us to take Lenny home. A short time later, Juliet told me that she'd met Stuart and Chloe one afternoon and they tearfully told her that their beautiful boy, Lenny, had died suddenly. Their poor dog was only three years old but had been struck down by a sudden and totally unexpected heart attack. What a tragedy to have struck at such a lovely family. Stuart so looked forward to coming home from university and spending time with Lenny and all the other dogs on the field. It just went to prove how unfair life can be at times. A few months later, Juliet was pleased to meet the brother and sister again with the newest addition to their family, a German Shepherd puppy, named Pippa. A happy ending all round to the 'Case of the disappearing Cassie.'

A final postscript to the story came when a phone call to the school encouraged them to repair the hole in their fence, which I'm pleased to say was quickly seen to, thus preventing similar occurrences in the future, not just by Cassie but any other dogs who might have felt a similar wanderlust.

Sunbathing

Chapter 10

Running, Jumping... Limping

As I'm sure you're all now quite aware of Cassie's insatiable love for running, jumping and playing in general, it came as a surprise to us, one day soon after her twelfth birthday, when we noticed one day that she was walking with a slight limp.

At first, we didn't think too much of it, as it certainly wouldn't have been the first time she'd over-exerted herself whilst running and playing on the field. We assumed at the time that it was probably a pulled muscle or something similar and we gave her a dose of Metacam, repeated for five days to help with any pain she might be feeling. When the five days had passed, her limp had actually grown more pronounced and in fact we could see that Cassie, though still happily running around and playing with her ball and her doggie friends, was holding her rear left leg off the ground so she was effectively running on three legs, with an occasional hop on the affected leg.

Clearly, we could see that this was more than a simple pulled muscle, so I phoned and made her an appointment with the vet. Two days later, Cassie was examined by Bernard at the surgery, and after testing her mobility reaction on that leg, he decided to carry out x-rays on it. She was booked in the following day and I dropped her off first thing in the morning. Because she required a general anaesthetic, I had to leave her at the vet's surgery and made arrangement to collect her at tea time. I felt so sorry for poor Cassie. Twelve years old, and we'd never left her with anyone else in all the years she'd lived with us. As the veterinary nurse led her from the examination room after I'd filled in the necessary consent form for the anaesthetic and x-ray procedure she looked at me with a look that seemed to say, *"Why are you going without me? Why can't I come home with you? I should be going for my walk and playtime now."* I had to walk away without looking back at her, not wanting her to get too stressed.

Why do dogs manage to make you feel like a mass murderer when you leave them at the vets? Quite obviously, if they've never been left there previously, they must think they're being abandoned. I couldn't help comparing Cassie's look of despair at me 'abandoning' her with the reaction of Sasha on the numerous occasions she's had to spend time at the surgery. Probably because she's been used to being treated there, for her two broken legs, numerous tests and in-patient treatment for her epilepsy, she's so used to spending time there that she seems to view it as her second home. Whenever I take her to the vet, Sasha gets excited as soon as we walk through the door and pulls me straight to the reception area where she goes through an elaborate greeting 'ceremony' to each of the staff on duty. She then tries to go through the door that leads to the treatment area, where she knows the rest of her friends are. The staff at the surgery have all known her since she was a tiny puppy and they all love her and call her 'their princess' so a vet visit is something Sasha enjoys, as opposed to poor Cassie who was about to be left for the first time, even if it was only for x-rays.

So, home I went, with the veterinary nurse who handled her admission assuring me the vet would phone me as soon as they had the results of the x-rays. Sure enough, I received the phone call from Bernard soon after 2 p.m. that afternoon. Cassie had ruptured the cruciate ligament in her right rear leg and would require surgery to repair it. Bernard went on to inform me of the different procedures available for her problem and I accepted his advice on the one he thought would be most suitable for our little dog. Juliet and I didn't hesitate of course. Cassie would have to undergo the operation if she was to have the chance of living what was for her a normal life of running and playing. Bernard assured me that she should have no problems returning to her usual self after a period of recuperation. Then he dropped the bombshell. Cassie would need to rest for SIX WEEKS after the operation. Can you imagine it? It was hard enough trying to keep Cassie still for more than a couple of minutes at the best of times, and here we were, faced with the prospect of trying to keep her off that leg and as still as possible for a month and a half!

We'd have to do our best of course and so Cassie was booked in for the operation the following week. Meanwhile, she continued on painkillers and, horror of horrors as far as she was concerned, she was restricted to short lead walks until she'd had her operation. No running, no jumping, no 'mad ferret' behaviour for Cassie until further notice. Can you imagine it? No? We couldn't either.

* * *

So, the fateful day arrived. Poor Cassie must have wondered why she wasn't allowed any breakfast for the second time in a week, having been starved since tea time the previous evening. When I clipped her lead on, she probably thought she was going for her usual morning walk. When, instead, I loaded her into the car, she must have wondered what was going on. We arrived at the surgery a little before 8.30 in the morning and were soon called through to the examination room where Cassie was weighed (she was all of 5.8 kilograms) and again, I had to complete the necessary paperwork, giving my consent for her to undergo the operation. Once again, it was arranged that I could collect her at tea time and I was given a specific collection appointment at 5 p.m.

I received a phone call soon after midday to let me know that the operation had been successfully carried out and that Cassie was doing well and in recovery. There was nothing more to be done except wait for five o'clock when I would make the journey to collect her and bring her home.

When I did go to pick her up I didn't have long to wait before I was called in to the treatment room. One of the nurses walked in carrying little Cassie in her arms. She looked so pathetic and forlorn, with her leg completely shaved, and a very large, self-adhesive bandage attached to it to cover the operation wound. Another bandage on her front leg, where the catheter had been inserted during her operation, completed the 'wounded soldier' look and poor Cassie, still quite dopey from the anaesthetic, looked utterly miserable, though her tail wagged a little bit when she saw me.

The nurse gently placed her on the examination table while she explained everything to me, regarding Cassie's post-operative care. Bernard, the vet had suggested she wear a 'buster' collar to prevent her from licking at the stitches on her leg, which at that time were covered by the large bandage. I explained the collar wouldn't be a good idea with all the other dogs in the house, as the others would make a bee-line for it and give Cassie no rest or peace because of the strange, 'alien' device attached to her head. Also, due to her little short legs, I envisioned her trying to eat or drink with the collar in place, and, recalling how difficult it had been for one of my dachshunds some years previously, I declined the collar and told the nurse we'd be ultra-vigilant in making sure she didn't gain access to the wound in order to lick it.

The nurse explained, as I was previously told in advance, that Cassie needed six weeks to recover from the procedure. There was to be no running, no jumping, (not even up on to the sofa or my armchair), and definitely no walks at all for at least the first two weeks. How on earth we were going to keep the mad ferret quiet and relatively still for two weeks initially, she didn't say, apart from suggesting keeping Cassie in a crate for her own safety and protection.

I knew that was definitely not an option. Juliet and I would watch her and care for her but there was no way we could envisage keeping her a virtual prisoner in a crate for two weeks, let alone six! Cassie would have ended up with serious psychological issues if we were to keep her imprisoned for any length of time.

* * *

I left the vet soon afterwards, armed with a new bottle of Metacam painkiller for Cassie and we were soon home, where Cassie, still quite groggy from the anaesthetic, was happy to flop into her bed in the lounge. It was the time of day when we allowed the rest of the dogs to join us in the lounge and they all seemed to sense Cassie's predicament. They each sniffed at her, and at her bandaged leg in particular, before wandering off and leaving her in peace, where she rested for the rest of the evening, only rising from her bed to go to the toilet at bedtime.

The following morning however, she appeared to have undergone an overnight transformation. She'd gone from looking and acting like a 'dead duck in a thunderstorm' to looking like... Cassie the mad ferret! She was jumping around (as much as she could on her three good legs), and acting perfectly normal, as much as was possible for her. When it came to 'walkies' time she began going wild, as if she expected to go for her normal walk, as if nothing unusual had happened.

"You've had an operation, you silly girl," I said. "You have to rest, Cassie." I might as well have been speaking to Henry the vacuum cleaner as far as Cassie was concerned. She just went on bouncing up and down and only stopped, so Juliet told me, when I disappeared through the back door with Sasha and Sheba, with whom she usually shared her morning walk. Once she realised we'd gone without her, Cassie appeared to go into a 'dog sulk' and went back to bed, but as soon as I returned with the two staffies, she was quickly back on her feet, trying to attract attention, as if to say, *"Now, is it my turn?"* You had to admire the little dog's determination and it was so tempting to give in to her, but her health came first and like it or not, Cassie would have to rest, as far as we could make her do so, and I can assure you, it wasn't easy. Every time Juliet or I took any of the dogs for a walk, Cassie would be there, scratching at the baby gate that kept her out of the kitchen, whining with her high-pitched little voice and peering through the bars, begging to go with us, but for now, she was confined to the lounge, only being allowed out into the garden for toileting purposes.

Three days after her operation she was back at the vets for her first post-operative check-up. The vet was delighted with her progress and laughed when I explained the problems she was causing. For him, it proved just how well she was doing. Originally he'd said Cassie could maybe have short, ten minute lead walks after four weeks, if she was doing okay but after seeing the progress she'd made in just three days, and after my explanation of her demeanour and behaviour since coming home, he revised that to say that if she had no problems, she could maybe have those short walks after two weeks, but he needed to see that she was starting to put some weight on her leg. So far, she was hopping around on three legs, carrying the injured one off the ground.

Sure enough, after two really fraught weeks, doing all we could to keep Cassie as rested as possible, Bernard the vet gave her the okay to begin short lead walks. She wasn't putting much weight on the leg yet, but at least she was trying. He hoped that by letting her walk on it, it would encourage her to put more weight on it, and help to build up some strength in the leg muscles.

Cassie was so excited the first time I put her lead on and led her out of the gate back into the big, wide world. Her tail was wagging and held high as I led her slowly along the street, and down the lane towards the church. I'd estimated it would take about ten minutes to reach the church and return home, so it would be the perfect walk for Cassie. She loved it, even though it was only for a few minutes. After the inactivity of the previous two weeks, she must have felt her life had begun again.

More check-ups continued over the next couple of weeks and her leg grew stronger with each passing day, until at last, she was putting most of her weight on it as she walked. Cassie was happy, I was happy and Bernard was happy, so much so that he gave her the all clear only four weeks after the operation, rather than the six weeks we'd expected. He specified one condition. Cassie could return to normal walks again as long as we promised to keep her on the lead for two weeks until she had a final check-up, and if all was okay at that time, she could be allowed to run and play again.

Everything went as planned and just six weeks after her operation, Cassie was back to running and playing as if nothing had ever happened to her. People were amazed to see her back so soon and so full of life. We had friends with dogs of their own who had undergone the same operation and had never been quite the same again afterwards. They, especially, were amazed at Cassie's powers of recuperation, especially at her age. While most dogs might be slowing down at the age of twelve, Cassie continued as fit and raring to go as she'd been when we first adopted her at the age of two.

Her fur soon grew back and before long there wasn't a single visible sign that Cassie had undergone surgery. With summer in full flow, Juliet gave her coat a nice even trim and her new growth on the leg quickly blended in with the shorter coat Juliet had given her during grooming, so she really looked amazing.

Cassie continued to go on amazing everyone who met her, with people meeting her for the first time still thinking she's a puppy rather than a grown dog.

"Twelve months old? Oh no, she's 'twelve YEARS old," was a typical reply from Juliet, though there were many people she met who thought she was even younger, still a young puppy.

Dogs really are quite remarkable as Cassie was soon back doing all the things she loves, and the operation soon became a thing of the distant past.

Cassie, post-op recovery

Chapter 11

Paws and Claws and Smelly Things

It's worth a couple of minutes to tell you about a few other things that make Cassie a little unusual. One of these is her teeth, or rather, lack of them! Right from the time we first adopted her, we noticed Cassie had unusual teeth, in as much as they were very short, and in some cases missing. We could only put it down to poor feeding and care when she was young. Looking back at the state she was in when our friend Linda first rescued her, it was logical to assume she hadn't been well fed and I'm pretty certain the old couple who first took her from Linda didn't think much about her teeth or their welfare. Looking closely at them you can easily imagine her, when in her early life, perhaps trying to bite her way through a fence or some other hard surface, and gradually grinding her teeth down.

Whatever the cause of her unusually configured teeth, it has never, ever stopped Cassie from enjoying a bone or anything else designed for dogs to chew on. In fact, there's nothing she loves better than a bone or something similar to chew on. When you consider the size of her mouth, (very small), it's a wonder she can open her jaws enough to fit even a small bone in her mouth, but, Cassie manages quite well.

I often wonder if the dogs she chases on the playing field are quite aware that the worst the little 'terrierist' chasing them along could do to them if she felt nasty would be to give them a thoroughly vicious suck!

Have I mentioned her coat previously? I might have done. But it's definitely worth mentioning again how she is transformed during the summer months, when Juliet gives her a really good clipping and her usually grey fluffy coat turns to a beautiful 'tiger-striped' design, with beautiful stripes of golden brown mixed in with her overall grey fur. Before most of our friends got used to seeing her like this, it wasn't entirely surprising that those who perhaps only saw her occasionally would sometimes ask Juliet or me if we had a new dog. They would then be surprised to be informed it was Cassie. Quite amazing what a difference a close trim can achieve in terms of a dog's appearance.

Now, I must tell you that Cassie absolutely hates being clipped. Juliet gets her on the grooming table and it then becomes a battle of wills as Cassie does her best to be uncooperative as Juliet attempts to make her look beautiful, no pampered pooch this one! Cassie could win the gold medal at the dog fidget Olympics! As for having her claws clipped, she's equally uncooperative, and it's a minor miracle that over the years, Juliet has always managed the task without drawing blood as our mad ferret pulls away or jumps about in her attempts to avoid the claw clippers. Juliet has lost count of the number of times she's received a quick nip, or a savage suck from those jaws as she's worked on the mad ferret, especially when trying to trim round her face. Then of course there's the tail, which Juliet doesn't trim too much, as it wouldn't look right if she was given a thin and wispy tail, but Cassie still finds reasons to object and does her best to whip round and try to nip Juliet or at the very least, the electric clippers.

As I'm typing this chapter, Juliet actually has Cassie on the grooming table, giving the little dog her summer trim. Sitting here in the kitchen I can hear everything that's happening in the utility room, which doubles as our home grooming parlour and so far, I've heard numerous expletives from Juliet, such as "You little s**t," as Cassie tries to nip her, "Keep still you crazy ferret," as she attempts to jump off the grooming table, and other terms of endearment, which I'm sure I can leave to your imagination.

Next of course, is Cassie's general anti-social attitude towards other humans. Though she can be so warm and loving with us at home, we noticed quite early in her life with us that she definitely has an aversion to being stroked or fussed by strangers. Because she looks so cute and cuddly, people are naturally attracted to her and will often try to give her a stroke or, even worse, a cuddle. Juliet or I have had to explain to so many people over the years that Cassie is not comfortable being fussed or stroked by people she doesn't know. She is even very selective with those she does know, including many people she's known for years. In her mind, Cassie probably has a list of highly privileged people who she will allow to approach her and touch her. We joke that she's a bit like the Queen, in as much as you can approach her, you can speak to her, but her body is inviolate. You can look but you must not touch! Now you may understand how fortunate it was for us that Stuart was obviously on her 'A' list on that day when she did her disappearing act into the ground so the local school. At least he was able to grab her and put her lead on when she was close enough. If it had been 99% of other people she would probably have just turned tail and run away in the opposite direction.

It's obviously disappointing for children sometimes who come up to Juliet and ask if the can "stroke the puppy" only to be told she doesn't like being touched. What makes us laugh is that if Juliet is walking Cassie with, let's say Digby and Muffin, who love to be stroked and cuddled, kids and even adults who don't know them will avoid them and won't ask if they can stroke them, even though they both love being stroked and cuddled. Could it be because they are staffy/springer crosses? Such a shame when people unwittingly show their breed prejudices in such a way.

When it comes to food, Cassie is again very set in her ways. She spends her daytime hours in the lounge with Penny, as I mentioned earlier in our story, and we also feed them in there at breakfast time. The evening meal is a different matter, as we have found over time that Cassie, the toothless wonder, eats her tea so fast that if we leave them together, she will devour her own food and then bully Penny out of the way and will then proceed to polish off the rest of poor Penny's tea. It's worth noting that Penny, at around 15 kilograms is more than twice Cassie's weight (6.5 kilos at the last weigh-in), and in overall size she is at least two to three times bigger than her daytime room-mate.

We found the solution to that little problem by feeding Cassie on her own in the lounge and Penny now has her tea in peace in the hall, near the front door, safely protected by the baby gate we use to stop the dogs getting to the stairs. Only four of them are allowed upstairs at bedtime, but never during the day.

* * *

I can't end this chapter without mentioning the 'smelly' part of the chapter title. I know, and you the reader will almost certainly know that dogs tend to be attracted to things that we humans regard as being foul-smelling. You know the sort of things I mean, fox poo, cow pats, that sort of thing. In Cassie's case, such disgusting pieces of other animals waste products act like a powerful magnet, becoming items that our 'cute' little dog simply can't resist rolling in, thus transforming her into a mobile canine sewage dump. Yesterday was a perfect example of my point. (As I write, it's June 2018). While on her afternoon walk with Juliet, Muffin and Petal, who were both behaving themselves, running and playing happily together, Cassie, as is quite normal, ran off to explore the nearby copses situated around the field. After a few minutes she reappeared and joyfully came bounding across the field, as fast as her little paws could carry her, looking very pleased with herself. As she drew closer, as Juliet told me a short time later when she returned home,

"I could smell her long before she reached me. She stunk to high heaven. When I saw her close up, I saw she was absolutely covered in brown slimy stuff, like some sort of liquid poo. It was all over her fur, her collar, everywhere."

Poor Juliet had left the offender on the front garden while she came in through the back door and gave Muffin and Petal to me. She then went out to attend to Madam Stinky. She did her best to get some of the stinking goo off her coat using a few baby wipes, and then took Cassie upstairs to give her a bath.

Now, giving Cassie a bath is not exactly the easiest job in the world. She tries to escape from the bath itself, slithers and sploshes around, and has the nasty habit of deciding to have a big shake halfway through the bath, soaking Juliet to the skin if she doesn't see it coming and gets out of the way in time. She may be tiny, but Cassie knows how to make her presence felt, especially where water is concerned. To make matters worse, she was so smelly yesterday that after rinsing her off with the shower, Juliet had to give her a second going over with the shampoo to remove any last, lingering traces of whatever it was that she'd succeeded in coating herself with.

Eventually, she was clean again, and Juliet gave her a quick towelling down and then left the heat of the day to finish her off. Juliet wouldn't have minded so much but she had already planned on grooming, clipping and bathing Cassie today, so the little wicked witch got a second dunking in the bath today. At least she's now the cleanest dog in the house!

Cassie's meerkat impersonation

Chapter 12

Ticks, Worms and Other Nasty Beasties

She may be small, she may be cute, but Cassie is, when all's said and done, a dog. As such, she is of course a target for all the usual pests and tiny predators that tend to plague our pet dogs lives. As responsible dog owners, we make sure that all our dogs are regularly 'wormed' to protect them from the usual suspects, tapeworm, ringworm etc.

For most of our dogs, this doesn't present a problem, but of course, most of our dogs aren't Cassie. While most of our dogs quite happily accept their worming tablets, either wrapped in a bit of cream cheese, or in some cases, mixed in with their food, three of our older dogs are extremely uncooperative at worming time.

Cassie, Dylan and Penny have all led Juliet and I a merry dance over the years when it comes to that time every six months. In the case of the mad ferret, we tried all sorts to get her to take her worming tablet, usually with little or no success. Whatever we did, no matter how we tried to disguise the one small tablet she must take, Cassie rejected it, and it ended up on the floor at her feet. Even burying the tablet in the middle of the meat portion of her tea was pointless. Cassie would quickly find it take it out and we'd find it on the floor beside her bowl after she'd finished her tea.

Thinking she wouldn't be able to reject it if we ground it up into a powder, we tried mixing the powder into her meal. Success? Not a hope! She just left the meal completely. It seemed she'd rather starve than take a worming tablet in any shape or form.

We'd try to give her the same meal the next day, this time smothering it in some lovely tasty gravy, made just for Cassie. She sniffed it, licked it, took a couple of mouthfuls, and then...turned away and left it again!

Exasperation was fast becoming the name of the game where Cassie and her worming tablet was concerned. In the end, I picked her up, led her in my arms, and Juliet opened her jaws, (the great white Cassie...hehe), and quickly inserted half a tablet into her mouth and using a plastic syringe, squirted water into her mouth, then held her mouth closed and massaged her throat until she felt Cassie swallow, and on checking, we found half a wormer had disappeared. Now all we had to do was get her to take the other half. As I'm sure you've realised by now, Cassie is quite an intelligent little dog, and she instantly realised what was about to happen as Juliet approached her with the other half of the tablet in her hand.

Cassie began squirming in my arms. "She knows," I said, stating the obvious.

"I know she knows," Juliet replied. "But she's going to take this other half if it kills me."

That was easier said than done of course. Apart from the fact she was now squirming like a worm on a hook in my arms, she also kept her jaws firmly clamped shut. Despite her diminutive size, Cassie showed how strong she was by resisting Juliet's efforts to prise her jaws open. Eventually, after numerous attempts, Juliet succeeded in opening Cassie's mouth and we followed the same procedure as before, and at long last, the wormer was gone, working its way towards Cassie's stomach, where it could do its job.

Obviously, we found it totally unacceptable to have to face such a struggle every time we needed to worm her, so before the next scheduled time for worming drew near, we put our heads together in an attempt to come up with a less stressful method of administering Cassie's worming tablet.

Around this time, we had begun serving Sasha's morning tablets in either a piece of cream cheese or wrapped in a small amount of Tesco's own brand of smooth pork liver paté. It was worth a try, so I cut the already small worming tablet into four tiny quarters and we once again set to work, trying to get Cassie to accept her 'special treat' from Juliet.

Cassie actually took the first piece from her hand but, just as we thought we'd hit on a successful method of tablet delivery, she suddenly spat out the tiny piece of tablet. Drat...foiled again. It was a case of back to the drawing board. Juliet and I were determined not to be outdone by our pint-sized little terrier. Somehow, we would find a way to get the worming tablet down without having to flush it down her throat, as before.

Time went by, and the battle to find a peaceful method of getting Cassie to accept her worming tablet dragged on as years passed. Whatever we tried, it seemed Cassie always knew when the wormers were on the menu. When we had to give her painkillers after her cruciate ligament operation we were grateful that the medication was in liquid form and could easily be given in her food.

It wasn't until introduced Sasha to a new diet to help with her epilepsy that we finally came up with the solution to the problem. Pilchards! Yes, after all those years of fighting and struggling to get the mad ferret to take her worming tablet the answer was there all the time, in the shape of the humble little fish, sold in tins in supermarkets all over the country.

We'd been advised to replace a large portion of Sasha's regular dog food with oily fish, usually pilchards and occasionally mackerel. These fish, high in Omega 3 oils had proved to be beneficial to dogs with canine epilepsy during a trial carried out by the Royal College of Veterinary Surgeons. One day, as worming time drew near again, I had a brainwave. Why not give Cassie some of the fishy flavoured tomato sauce from Sasha's pilchards with the worming tablet crushed up in it? Surely even Cassie wouldn't be able to sniff it out amongst the strong combined smell of fish and tomato sauce. Juliet thought about it and said, "Well, as she's getting on a bit, and she's had that trouble with her back leg, why not go one step further and give her an actual pilchard with her tea? The Omega 3 oils with be good for her and together, the taste and smell of the fish and the juice should mask the wormer."

"Good idea," I replied. "If this doesn't work, we'll be pretty much back to square one."

So, time for a drum roll, folks. Doggie tea time came around. I crushed up Cassie's little tablet. I mixed it in with a pilchard and plenty of the nice tomato sauce from the tin and mixed it all in with her regular dog food, and...EUREKA! She ate the lot, and Juliet and I were ecstatic. After years of fighting and struggling with her to try and get something as simple as a worming tablet down her throat, we'd finally found the winning formula. Thank God for pilchards in tomato sauce. Of course, we've stuck to that procedure ever since and we no longer have a problem with Cassie and her wormers, though we did have similar problems with Dylan and Penny.

Guess what? Yes, after succeeding with Cassie and the pilchards, we tried the same thing with the other two problem tablet-takers and met with instant success. Worming time has now become less stressful as none of our other dogs have a problem with taking their tablets. Peace reigns supreme at worming time!

* * *

One little 'nasty' that Cassie is regularly plagued with are those horrible sticky little buds that are like tiny burrs that stick to the fur of long-haired dogs. Cassie having soft, longish fur and being so close to the ground, is especially prone to getting them stuck to her fur when out on a walk or while running and playing on grass. Those things affect Dylan too. When either of them comes home from a walk in the summer, it can often take Juliet or me up to half an hour to work our way through their coats, slowly removing each of those little burrs by hand, one at a time. It's the only way to get them off without pulling their fur out and hurting them. Of course, where there's grass there is always the possibility of something even nastier than sticky buds to watch out for and Cassie has twice been attacked by horrible ticks. The first time, two years ago, we weren't sure at first just what it was. Juliet had come home from a walk and I bent down to give Cassie a stroke and remove her lead.

As I ran my hand down her back I felt something sticking up between her shoulder blades. Thinking she might have got a thorn stuck in her fur from all the ferreting around in the bushes, I took a closer look.

"Juliet, come and take a look," I said as I realised what it was. "I think Cassie's got a tick."

"Yes, she has," my wife confirmed. "We'd better get rid of it quickly."

Fortunately, our doggie first aid box, that we'd built up over the years, contained a tick remover, though we'd never had cause to use it up until that day. As usual, nothing was quite as simple as it should have been where Cassie was concerned. Our mad ferret saw the first aid box being taken from the drawer where we kept it in the utility room, and, as if she knew exactly what was about to happen, the crafty little terrier did her best to quietly sneak off into the next room. I saw what she was doing and quickly closed the baby gate that allows us to seal off the kitchen from the utility room if necessary.

"Come on, Cassie Lou," I said, using another of our little nicknames for her. "We need to get rid of that nasty thing before it can cause an infection and make you a poorly little girl."

Cassie looked up at me as if she understood what I was saying. Maybe it was the gentle, soothing sound I put into my voice to reassure her, and she came to me and allowed me to pick her up. Being so tiny, it wasn't a practical course of action for Juliet or me to get down on our knees to try and remove the tick while she stood on the floor. We'd never get her to stand still long enough to do the job.

While I held her in my arms, Juliet approached her with the tick removing tool, a long plastic arm with a wire loop at the end, suitable for fitting over the exposed part of the nasty little beastie. Cassie decided, on a matter of principal, to make the job more difficult than it needed to be by beginning to squirm in my arms.

"Hold her still," Juliet ordered me.

"I'm trying to, but she's wriggling about too much."

"Keep still, Cassie," she ordered. As if the mad ferret was going to take any notice of that!

Eventually, I got Cassie to keep relatively still in my arms and, following the instructions of the packaging of the tick remover, she slipped the tool over the exposed part of the tick, and then, by exerting a small amount of pressure on the arm of the tool, she closed the wire loop over the body and tightened it as firmly as possible. It was important, the instructions said, to ensure the whole tick was removed and no parts were left in the dog's body, so first of all Juliet had to ensure she didn't tighten the wire loop too much in case it sliced through the tick, leaving it's feeding parts under the skin, which would almost certainly lead to infection. Now came the 'icky' bit. Using a firm but gentle twisting action, and pulling upwards at the same time, Juliet gradually pulled the little bloodsucker out of Cassie's body. As it came clear of Cassie's back we were both surprised at the size of it. It was smaller than we expected, and difficult to imagine just how much damage it could have caused if it had been left to feed on Cassie's blood without being removed.

Removing the tick was only the first stage of the process, however. Having removed it from Cassie's body the important thing was now to dispose of it. It had to be killed in order to stop it from attaching itself to another dog or animal of some description. Holding it in the wire loop, I took the tick outside and released the loop, placing it on the ground in front of me. It isn't always possible to kill a tick just by standing on it, the instructions clearly explained. It was essential to crush it with something heavy, so I asked Juliet to pass me a hammer from my tool drawer. I then gave the offending parasite a mighty 'whack' with the hammer and I could have sworn I heard its blood gorged body go 'pop' as the hammer extinguished its life. Not wanting to take any chances, I then washed down the paving slab where I'd done the deed with boiling water and bleach to ensure no trace of the offending tick remained.

In all the years we've lived here, this was our first encounter with one of these nasty little bloodsucking parasites, perhaps surprisingly. Yet, just a few months later, Cassie went and got herself another one! It could only have happened to our mad ferret. Luckily, we were now well acquainted with the procedure for removing the little pests, and this time, Cassie appeared much more cooperative and we were able to remove this one with much less fuss than we'd encountered from her with the first one. We soon disposed of the second tick and much to our relief, Cassie has never been bothered with them since then and nor have any of our other dogs.

* * *

One pest that has never really bothered Cassie or any of our dogs, is fleas. Considering we have eleven dogs, you might find that quite surprising, as we did at one time. We can only surmise that regular grooming and constant vigilance have combined to keep our home a no-go zone where fleas are concerned. I recall one year, one of our dogs, (not Cassie) was found to have a small flea problem, but fast administration of a flea killing medication dealt with the problem in less than twenty four hours. A second problem did raise its head with another of our dogs some time later was dealt with in a similar manner and we've remained a 'flea-free zone' ever since.

It really is quite incredible that Cassie has now reached the grand old age of fourteen years and has had so few problems with her health or with the common parasites that affect dog's lives. Her story, however is not quite over as this year, she decided to give us cause for concern once again.

Chapter 13

Here We Go Again

As 2017 drew to a close, and Christmas approached, we were surprised when one evening my youngest stepdaughter, Victoria, arrived home from college one evening and said to Juliet,

"Mum, you need to come outside now, please."

"Why, what's wrong?" Juliet replied.

"Nothing's wrong. I just need you to come outside for a minute."

Juliet, not too pleased at being dragged away from what she was doing, followed Victoria outside and I wondered what could have happened. A couple of minutes later, Juliet walked back into the house carrying... a puppy!

The tiny bundle was wrapped up in a blanket and Victoria followed closely behind her mum with a comfy small dog bed and a bag containing a couple of dog toys, a cuddly toy and a few other items needed for a new puppy.

The puppy was very cute and beautiful as puppies usually are, but Juliet and I were quite angry with Victoria at first. She's often asked if we could have a puppy over the last few months and both Juliet and I had explained to her that we didn't want any more dogs. After all, we're not getting any younger and some of our dogs are already the canine equivalent of old age pensioners, so the last thing any of us needed was a new puppy and all the work that went with it, in terms of training, feeding, house training, lead training, socialisation, and anything else you can think of associated with caring for a new pup.

Victoria insisted the puppy was her Christmas present to her mum, and she could hardy take it back to where she'd bought it, could she? She'd been saving her wages from her part-time job in order to buy the dog. She had us well and truly ensnared, as she knew she would. The puppy, who she told us was called Honey was in fact a beautiful honey-coloured cross breed that Victoria said was a Staffy/Jack Russell Cross. We've since come to doubt that lineage as the longer we've had Honey, (she's almost 9 months old at the time of writing), the longer she's grown, though she doesn't seem to be growing any taller. Juliet and I are convinced there's some dachshund in there, somewhere. When people meet her for the first time, and ask what breed she is, we now jokingly reply, "She's a draught-excluder terrier." Well, she is quite good at keeping draughts out if she lies across the bottom of a door.

All the dogs accepted the little puppy into the family from day one, with Sasha especially finding a special place for Honey in her affections, and in fact, she immediately 'adopted', Sasha becoming a kind of surrogate mother, much as she did some years ago when we last brought puppies into the house. On that occasion, she adopted Muffin, Petal, and Digby, who all arrived from the same litter, from the moment they arrived in our home.

Did I say all the dogs accepted Honey from the start? Well, there was one small exception to that statement. Little Cassie, who was bigger than Honey when she first arrived, seemed a little slower than the others in accepting her new pack-mate. Perhaps it was something to do with the fact that here at last was another dog that actually competed with her when it came to the boundless energy stakes. Honey, as most puppies probably are, was so full of life and energy that she could quickly wear out any of the other dogs that played with her, though Sasha was able to control her, much as her real mother would have done, and when Sasha had had enough, she'd let Honey know by her body language and the puppy knew it was time to stop.

As time has gone by, and Honey has continued to grow, she quickly overtook Cassie in size, and now, at almost nine months old at the time of writing, Honey stands at around 13 kilograms while Cassie remains somewhere in the region of 6.5 kilos, hardly a heavyweight. Maybe that's why, of all the dogs, Cassie seems to give Honey something of a wide berth, as though she is slightly afraid of the newcomer, though fear wouldn't be the right word to use. I seriously don't think Cassie fears any dog, so maybe she just maintains a healthy respect for little Honey.

Puppy Honey

* * *

The phrase 'no fear' certainly jumps into my mind when I describe the latest incident in Cassie's life, one that has seen her having to go under the surgeon's knife again.

It all began one evening as we were all relaxing us usual in the lounge. Suddenly, out of nowhere or so it seemed, two of the dogs, Digby and Sheba decided to have a fall-out. As anyone who owns multiple dogs will know, such minor altercations are quite common and can usually be described as being like 'handbags at dawn' in terms of severity. Juliet and I were sort of half-asleep when the incident began, it being near to bedtime and both of us being very tired after a long day. We both jumped up from our seats and moved to separate the two dogs who were 'fighting' like a pair of Sumo Wrestlers, more than a pair of prize-fighters, with a lot of posturing and holding on to each other without biting or causing any damage. In other words, it was much ado about nothing, or rather it would have been if we didn't suddenly notice, underneath the two squabbling dogs…yes, you've guessed it, Cassie! Somehow, our own mad ferret had leapt in to the fray and got herself caught up underneath the two sparring staffies. If it hadn't been so dangerous for her it would have been funny. There she was, throwing herself into the middle of an argument between two much larger dogs, with no thought for the fact that she was nowhere near their size or strength.

As we separated the two larger dogs, Cassie suddenly shot out from underneath them and either from fear, (?) or panic, she dashed out of the room at top speed and took advantage of the fact the baby gate at the bottom of the stairs wasn't fully closed and she ran up the stairs at top speed, and was gone in a flash. I went upstairs to find her and was totally surprised to find her on our bed. How on earth she'd managed to jump up to the height of our bed I'll never know but considering what we later discovered, the leap she made must have been a factor in what followed.

I picked her up and carried her downstairs, and when I put her down on the floor we saw a couple of cuts, or little bite marks on her, where she'd managed to get herself caught under the two warring dogs, both of whom were totally unscathed of course.

"Silly girl, Cassie," I said to her, and then, as she toddled away out in to the garden, I noticed she was walking with a slight limp. Juliet and

I figured that she'd probably pulled a muscle or tendon in her flight up the stairs and we decided to keep a close watch on her for the next couple of days to see how her leg progressed.

Over the following few days, Cassie's limp, far from improving, appeared to grow more pronounced. I had the niggling fear that we'd been here before and that Cassie could have damaged her cruciate ligament, this time in her right leg. We decided to give it a couple more days and if we saw no sign of improvement, we'd take her to the vet, which of course, I ended up doing three days later.

The vet examined her closely, very closely, and decided that x-rays were required to confirm the diagnosis, but yes, she agreed with my assessment that in all likelihood, Cassie had cruciate ligament damage. I arranged to take her back first thing the next day, when Cassie would be anaesthetised for the x-rays to be taken. When I picked her up later that day, her vet showed me the x-rays, and the diagnosis was confirmed.

She explained that the x-rays had been forwarded to the consulting orthopaedic surgeon in Manchester, who had agreed with the diagnosis. Unfortunately, the damage to Cassie's ligament was quite extensive and would require implants in her leg to help to correct the damage, so it would be a different operation to the one she'd undergone two years previously.

"It could only happen to Cassie," Juliet exclaimed when I explained it all to her.

"I know," I agreed. "I've booked her in for the op next Wednesday. It's the first day the surgeon can come over from Manchester. We must have her there by 8.15 in the morning and he's put her first on his list. The vet did stress that, due to Cassie's age, there is a higher risk attached to the operation, as she'll be under the anaesthetic for quite a while, but the surgeon says he's confident she'll be okay due to her incredible fitness levels. Plus, if we don't have it done, she's going to be in pain and lame for the rest of her life."

"We've got to have it done," Juliet agreed. "Can you imagine how miserable and unhappy Cassie would be if she couldn't run and play?"

So that was it, all agreed. Of course, we couldn't help agreeing that it could all have been avoided if Cassie hadn't decided to go into 'mad ferret' mode and dive into action when the two bigger dogs were having their altercation. They must have at least given her a fright, because she wouldn't normally even try to go up the stairs, to a part of the house she's not allowed access to. Either running up the stairs at full speed on her little tiny legs, or making what was an incredible leap for a dog her size, onto our bed, had obviously done the damage. That was just typical of Cassie's luck. She was unscathed from getting involved in Digby and Sheba's fall-out, but managed to rupture her ligament while running away!

In the meantime, until the day of her operation, she was restricted to short lead walks and was on painkillers. Already banned from any running and jumping, our little Cassie was clearly depressed and we couldn't wait for the following Wednesday to come around so the healing process could begin... again!

Chapter 14

Operation Cassie

The Wednesday came around soon enough and off I went at 8 a.m. with Cassie in the back of the car. We'd changed our car since the first operation and I must say, she looked very miniscule and quite pathetic in the rear luggage area of our Citroën Xsara Picasso. Being early in the day, traffic was light, so the journey to the veterinary surgery only took about ten minutes. Cassie was called in almost immediately upon our arrival and I signed the various documentation to allow the operation to go ahead. I couldn't help experiencing a feeling of déjà vu as I once again walked out of the surgery, minus our little Cassie. Once again, she'd looked so pathetic as I left her, with the nurse holding her lead, and her little tail suddenly stopped wagging as she realised I wasn't taking her with me.

I felt so guilty, even though I was doing something that would ultimately help her. Seeing how Cassie reacted to me leaving her that morning also brought to my mind another thought, totally unrelated to that days' events, or, was it? It was the thought that I, like I'm sure many of you, also, read so many stories on social media about dogs being taken to shelters or rescue centres and being dumped there by uncaring owners. I'm not talking about the ones who have no choice through financial hardship, or serious health issues making it difficult for the owner to care for their dog, but I mean the ones where a dog is getting on in years and for no good reason its owners decide they can longer be bothered with caring for it, and so they simply abandon their dogs to their fate, often leaving them at high-kill shelters (in the USA), where they should know their dog will in all likelihood be put to sleep rather than re-homed. I say again, how can they do such things? I was going to be getting our Cassie back in a few hours and yet, just seeing the look on her face that morning left me feeling like a mass murderer, suffering from a heavy bout of remorse and guilt. Heavy stuff huh?

So, I was sitting by the phone after lunch, the vet having promised I would hear from them when the operation was concluded and Cassie was conscious again. When the vet called the news was good, and it felt like a great weight had lifted from my shoulders. I admit, I was more worried than I'd thought about Cassie having the operation because of her age, but, she's a tough little girl and had come through it all okay.

I picked her up later that evening and it was back to the same routine as with her previous cruciate ligament operation, six weeks rest, and no walks until the vet was happy she could put significant weight on her leg. Like the last time, Cassie was very groggy from the anaesthetic at first and probably because it was a more complicated operation, she took longer to fully recover from it. She spent the first two days after the operation resting in her bed, which was a surprise to us, but a good one, really, as it meant she was getting the rest she required.

The third day saw a big difference, however as, when we came down the stairs first thing in the morning, little Cassie was already up and about, albeit on three legs, toddling around the lounge where she was clearly in search of breakfast! She'd hardly eaten a thing for two days, and only then when we literally put her food bowl in her bed next to her. Now, she was looking more like our Cassie again and she really devoured her breakfast. As had happened previously, Cassie improved by leaps and bounds, figuratively speaking as it would be a few weeks until she was given the all-clear to run and play again.

Despite what had happened to her, Cassie showed no nervousness or fear when reintroduced to the rest of the dogs. As always, her mega attitude saw Cassie quickly reassert herself when the rest of the pack were allowed into the lounge in the evenings. Instead of secreting herself in her usual place under the coffee table, she'd taken up the bed we kept next to my armchair, where Sasha usually spent the evening snoozing close to me. If any dog, including Sasha, encroached on the space around the bed, she would growl or give them one of her trademark barks, more like a screech really, and everyone soon learned to leave her in peace as she slowly recuperated.

After the previous operation, Juliet and I felt like a pair of old hands at managing her recovery, and it wasn't long before she once again got the all-clear to resume short lead walks, and a couple of weeks later, the vet pronounced her fit enough to return to normal activities, as long as her running was limited to short spells to begin with. Cassie was so happy and as soon as she was allowed off her lead on the playing field after a six-week absence, it was as if she'd never been away. Her legs just flew over the grass as she ran her heart out with the sheer joy of being able to run and play again. It was so good to see her enjoying her life again.

It was around this time that a friend of mine on Facebook, Kath Bradbury, made an extremely generous gesture which Cassie benefitted from. Having bought a new dog coat for her dog, Poppy, Kath found it was too small for her dog and knowing we had a number of dogs, kindly asked me if it would be suitable for one of our doggie family. I was so touched by her generosity and very grateful when she sent the coat to me and it proved to be a perfect fit for little Cassie. It was a lovely gesture and one Juliet and I certainly won't forget in a hurry.

We hoped Cassie might have learned a lesson from the latest incident, and maybe keep out of the way in future if any of the bigger dogs had a disagreement. Unfortunately, Cassie just can't keep her little nose out of other people's (or dog's) business as the latest incident to befall our mad ferret illustrates.

* * *

It was a beautiful sunny morning, just yesterday. Cassie asked to go out, needing the toilet, so I let her out into the back garden with me and a few of the other dogs. A while later, Juliet arrived home with Muffin, Digby and Honey, who'd been for their morning walk. As she walked through the gate, Cassie began to 'kick-off' with a series of her distinctive barks. For some reason this seemed to spark a disagreement between Digby and Muttley who engaged in what I would describe as another of those 'handbags at dawn' type of fall out. They looked like a pair of boxing kangaroos. Looking back, we are pretty sure that the current heatwave was a contributing factor in what took place as the heat is certainly making not just dogs, but people quite 'cranky' at present.

If Cassie had kept away we would have quickly separated them and the matter would have ended there, but no, Cassie, as always believing herself to be as big and tough as the other dogs, decided to get involved and flew in to join the fray. Before we knew it she was somehow dragged under Digby and Muttley and was screeching her high-pitched panic scream. By the time we'd managed to extricate her from the situation, she was covered in numerous bites and scratches, mostly quite small but there were a couple of larger bites that concerned us greatly. Digby had a scratch on his face and Muttley had a loose tooth. As always seems to happen, poor Cassie had come off worst.

Cassie of course would need urgent vet treatment as she was bleeding quite a lot. I phoned the vet who advised me to take them both in right away. I was already blaming myself, as Cassie of course usually spends most of the day in the lounge with little Penny, but of course, I had to let her out if she needed to go to the toilet.

Juliet quickly wrapped Cassie in a large bath sheet and we loaded her and Muttley into the back of the Citroën. A ten-minute drive and we were at the vets, where we were seen immediately. They were seen by the senior vet, the practice manager who, quite sensibly stated that we couldn't and shouldn't blame the other dogs for Cassie's injuries. As Rebecca said to me at the time, "Dogs fight sometimes. In ten minutes they are usually best friends again. We all know what Cassie's like and she doesn't understand she's less than half the size of Muttley and Digby."

After so many years as dog rescuers and owners we would never have blamed the other dogs anyway, (apart from the one time, years ago, with Sheba when we were really still learning how to handle a pack of dogs), but it was nice to have that reassurance from a senior vet.

Of course, I had to leave both dogs at the surgery. Cassie needed multiple stitches and Muttley required some stitches to his gum and his canine tooth removing. Having lost one of his canine teeth a couple of years ago this means that our poor Muttley is now 'fangless' as Juliet put it. I returned home where we spent a worrying few hours waiting for news about our two in-patient dogs. When the phone call came from the vets, it was with mixed news.

Later that day, I was able to bring Muttley home, but had to take Cassie to the overnight vets for observation. Her operation had taken place later in the day and she was still on fluids at the time the vet closed so an overnight stay was recommended. So, as I collected Muttley, I was faced with the drive across town to the 'out of hours' vet surgery, where Cassie would spend the night under observation. Having been to the Emergency Overnight Surgery three years ago when Sasha was seriously ill after suffering thirteen epileptic seizures in 24 hours, I knew my way and also knew Cassie would receive the best of care from the vet and staff at the overnight facility. I called the clinic just before going to bed at midnight to check on her condition and was informed by the veterinary nurse who replied to my call that Cassie was doing just fine and had eaten not one but TWO dinners later that evening. Sounded like she was doing great to me.

I returned to the overnight clinic at 7.30 the following morning to collect her and took her directly to our vet for her to be examined again. I had to leave her once more as they wanted her to have plenty of rest and more painkillers, but there was a chance I could bring her home later in the evening. It was a long, hot day, as the summer heatwave is quite relentless this year and it was almost impossible to cool down or relax properly as I waited once again for the phone call that would tell me whether I could collect Cassie and bring her home that evening. When the call came, it was good news, and I was informed I could collect Cassie at 6pm.

After receiving the phone call, time seemed to pass a little faster and it was soon time to return to the vet surgery and this time I was able to bring Cassie home, as she'd made such good progress during the day. I had very strict instructions however, and we had to keep her quiet and rested, which, due to the painkillers she'd been given, wasn't too difficult, as she was very dopey and couldn't really stand up unaided. As the vet explained,

"The meds we've given her are quite strong, so she'll probably be seeing pink elephants at the moment."

I phoned Juliet from the surgery and asked her to place Cassie's bed in the hall at home, so we could keep her isolated for the first evening at home, so she could get plenty of rest. Once we were all ready for bed we could move her bed into the lounge where she could spend the night in her usual place, with just Penny for company.

As planned, Cassie spent a peaceful evening in her bed, and at bed-time we went through our usual routine, with all the dogs being let out in the back garden before bed. With the others all settled in their beds, Juliet and I set off for bed, accompanied by Muffin, Petal and Digby, and of course, Sasha who all sleep in our bedroom. The others all went straight past Cassie in her bed, but Sasha stopped and bent down, tail wagging, as if to give Cassie a little doggie kiss. Imagine our surprise when Cassie suddenly bared her teeth and reached up and gave Sasha a quick high-pitched bark in her face, making poor Sasha jump back in shock. We couldn't believe it. Here was Cassie, just back from the vets, looking like she'd gone ten rounds with Mike Tyson, and she still couldn't resist telling Sasha off for encroaching on her space. We had to laugh. Our 'Mad Ferret' was well and truly home!

Cassie has since returned to the vet again for two post-op checks and I'm delighted to say the vet was really pleased with her. She's having to wear a sort of body bandage at present, but this is just to help prevent infection in her wounds.

The veterinary nurses, who are all madly in love with Cassie (*"Isn't she a quiet little soul?"*) think she's absolutely the 'bees knees' but this is the very first time I've heard Cassie described as *quiet*. Each time I've taken her in so far, they've had fun 'dressing her up' in a different patterned body bandage on each occasion. The most recent one has a giraffe skin pattern, whilst she has previously had a floral print one and a general wildlife design. I have to admit that Cassie has been the perfect patient at the surgery, though they are all astounded when I tell them that at home, Cassie just hasn't changed one little bit and is still determined to rule the roost and is back to telling everyone off if they encroach on her space. Of course, this makes Juliet and I quite nervous after all that's happened and we now know we are going to have to watch Cassie very closely in future for her own safety and security.

In a week or two, the vet has promised that Cassie can return to life as normal; her stitches will all be removed and she will once again be set loose upon the village playing fields, where once again, and for the foreseeable future, Cassie, the mad ferret and wicked witch of the west will once again be running, chasing, ball-stealing and in general, being the source of great fun and amusement to us, and to everyone who knows her, or meets her for the first time.

By the time you read this, her story so far, I'm sure she will be back to her best, and Cassie's story will go on for a long time to come. She may be getting on in years, but there's no sign of her slowing down or changing her attitude towards the other, bigger dogs, so it seems that as far as Cassie's concerned, she's still 'the boss' and it appears to those of us who know and love her, she always will be.

A present from Kath and Poppy

Chapter 15

The Future?

As we all know, it's impossible to accurately predict the future, but in Cassie's case there are some things that are certain. Our daily 'management' of her place in our home will continue unchanged. She will go on spending her daytimes in the lounge with Penny, where the pair will be joined frequently by me and Sasha as I do a lot of my writing sitting on the sofa, Sasha by my side.

As for the evenings, we've already introduced a stricter regime as we wouldn't want Cassie performing her 'Moray eel' act on the bigger dogs any longer in case any of them take exception to her 'bullying' of them. So, Cassie is now banned from secreting herself under the coffee table and is quite happy spending her evenings either in her bed beside my chair, or cuddled up on my chair beside me, which she loves as of course she gets lots of love and cuddles that way.

Of course she will still need to use the garden to go to the toilet during the day, but to ensure there can be no chance of a repeat of the recent incident, when we let her out the other dogs will be confined in the house and she will only be allowed to share her garden time with the smaller dogs, such as Dylan and Penny, and of course, Sasha, who is like a 'mother hen' and who loves sitting watching over any of her pack mates like a guardian angel. No chance of anything happening if we keep her isolated from the main body of the pack.

I mustn't finish Cassie's story without saying a big thank you to Rebecca and the nurses and staff at Vets for Pets in Doncaster, who have cared for Cassie for the last twelve years, and especially for the love and care shown towards her with relation to her current injuries.

To all dog lovers and owners who may read this book, let me just say that one of the most important factors in keeping dogs, and in providing them with the best possible care at all times, is…insurance! The current bill for Muttley and Cassie's treatment is likely to exceed £2,000. That's not small change in anybody's book and of course, we always keep all our dogs insured because as this latest incident as proved to us, you just never know when you will need the cover provided by a reputable pet insurance company. Not only can good insurance cover help to lessen the trauma and stress any owner will feel when they are worrying about their pet's health and well-being, but it can also help to prevent any owner having to make the heart-breaking decision to have their much-loved pet put to sleep simply because they didn't think they needed to insure them. Believe me when I say I've seen too many grieving dog owners who fell victim to what I call the *'It'll never happen to me'* syndrome. For the sake of a few pounds or dollars a week your dog can be covered against almost any eventuality and you can sleep well at night knowing you won't have to face that awful decision if you don't have the money to pay for your dog's veterinary treatment.

So, back to Cassie and her future. By now, I'm sure you know that there really isn't much Juliet and I can do to change the personality of our very special little 'mad ferret' and we certainly wouldn't want to. Cassie is quite remarkable to have reached the grand old age of fourteen years and to still want to run and play and romp with other dogs no matter how big they may be, and to have no fear of anything, man or beast. It's going to be up to us as loving and responsible owners to make sure she's allowed to do all those things for as long as she's with us, but in a safely controlled way that will hopefully mean fewer and fewer vet visits for our little girl in the future.

She's a very special little dog, who we love and cherish very much, so I can only close by saying this certainly isn't the end of Cassie's Tale, but maybe best described as being the end of the beginning of a story that I'm sure still has many chapters that may have to be added a year or two from now. For now though, both Cassie and I thank you for reading the story of her life so far. We've loved sharing her life with you all.

I hope you'll come back and see us again when I write the next book in my rescue dog series, though I've still to decide on which of our dogs to feature next. If you've enjoyed Cassie's Tale please be kind enough to leave a short review of the book on Amazon. Good reviews are so important and vital in helping the book to reach a wider audience.

To see my other books, including the award-winning Sasha and Sheba: From Hell to Happiness, please visit my website at http://www.brianlporter.co.uk/ and for regular posts about our family of rescuedogs, you can visit Sasha's Facebook page at https://www.facebook.com/harry.porter.12139862

You're also invited to visit my Amazon author page at https://www.amazon.co.uk/Brian-L.-Porter/e/B00466KITC

Our family of dogs

About the Author

Brian L Porter is an award-winning, bestselling author, whose books have regularly topped the Amazon Best Selling charts. Writing as Brian, he has won a Best Author Award, and his thrillers have picked up Best Thriller and Best Mystery Awards. The third book in his Mersey Mystery series, *A Mersey Maiden* recently won The Best Book We've Read all Year Award, from Readfree,ly.

When it comes to dogs and dog rescue he is passionate about the subject and his two previous dog rescue books have been hugely successful. Sasha: A Very Special Dog Tale of a Very Special Epi-Dog is now an award-winning international bestseller and Sheba: From Hell to Happiness is also a UK Bestseller and an award winner too. Cassie's Tale is the third book in the series and there are sure to be more to follow.

Writing as Harry Porter his children's books have achieved three bestselling rankings on Amazon in the USA and UK.

In addition, his third incarnation as romantic poet Juan Pablo Jalisco has brought international recognition with his collected works, *Of Aztecs and Conquistadors* topping the bestselling charts in the USA, UK and Canada.

Brian lives with his wife, children and of course, Sasha and the rest of his wonderful pack of ten rescued dogs.

A Mersey Killing and the following books in his Mersey Mystery series have already been optioned for adaptation as a TV series, in addition to his other novels, all of which have been signed by ThunderBall Films in a movie franchise deal.

Other Books by the Author

Dog Rescue Series
Sasha – A Very Special Dog Tale of a Very Special Epi-Dog
Sheba: From Hell to Happiness

Thrillers by Brian L Porter
A Study in Red - The Secret Journal of Jack the Ripper
Legacy of the Ripper
Requiem for the Ripper
Pestilence
Purple Death
Behind Closed Doors
Avenue of the Dead
The Nemesis Cell
Kiss of Life

The Mersey Mystery Series
A Mersey Killing (Amazon bestseller)
All Saints, Murder on the Mersey
A Mersey Maiden
A Mersey Mariner
A Very Mersey Murder
(Coming soon) – Last Train to Lime Street
(Coming soon) – A Mersey Ferry Tale

Short Story Collections
After Armageddon (Amazon bestseller)

Remembrance Poetry
Lest We Forget (Amazon bestseller)

Children's books as Harry Porter
Wolf (Amazon bestseller)
Alistair the Alligator, (Illustrated by Sharon Lewis) (Amazon bestseller)
Charlie the Caterpillar (Illustrated by Bonnie Pelton) (Amazon bestseller)

As Juan Pablo Jalisco
Of Aztecs and Conquistadors (Amazon bestseller)

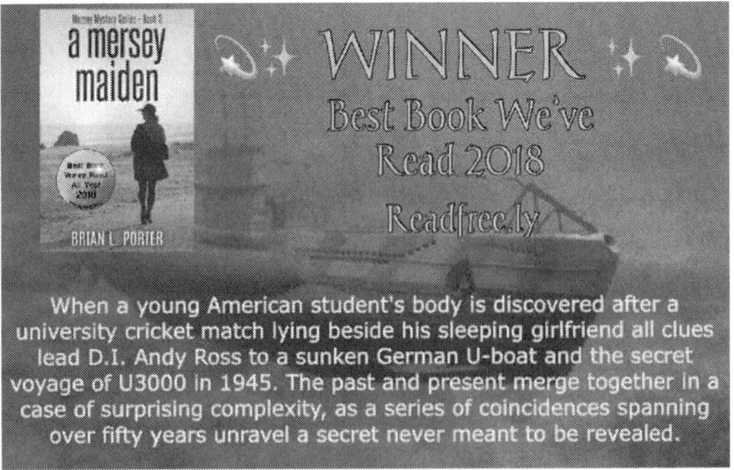

Printed in Great Britain
by Amazon

36600136R00066